P9-DDF-642

EASY MOSAICS

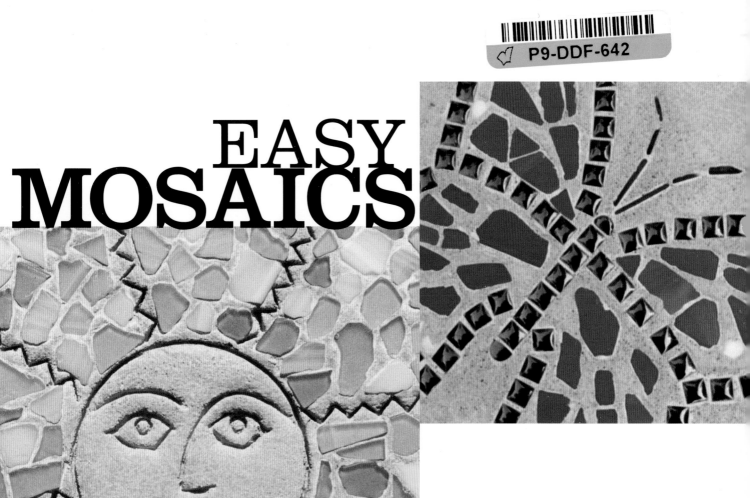

for your **home and garden**

sarah donnelly

NORTH LIGHT BOOKS

CINCINNATI, OHIO

www.artistsnetwork.com

Dedication

To Candy Moger, "My Naber", who always has good tea, a great eye, and time to listen to my latest crazy idea.

A NOTE ABOUT SAFETY

The author and publisher disclaim any liability for damages or injury resulting from the use of this information.

Easy Mosaics for Your Home and Garden. © 2001 by Sarah Donnelly. Manufactured in China. All rights reserved. No part of this book may be reproduced in any form or by any electronic or mechanical means including information storage and retrieval systems without permission in writing from the publisher, except by a reviewer, who may quote brief passages in a review. Published by North Light Books, an imprint of F&W Publications, Inc., 1507 Dana Avenue, Cincinnati, Ohio 45207. (800) 289-0963. First edition.

Other fine North Light Books are available from your local bookstore or art supply store or direct from the publisher.

05 04 03 02   5 4 3 2

Library of Congress Cataloging-in-Publication Data

Donnelly, Sarah, 1955-
    Easy mosaics for your home and garden / by Sarah Donnelly.
        p.cm.
    Includes index.
        ISBN 1-58180-129-7 (alk. paper)
        1. Mosaics—Technique. 2. Handicraft. I. Title.

    TT910 .D66 2001
    738.5'2--dc21

                                    20011032634

Editor: Maggie Moschell
Designer: Stephanie Strang
Production coordinator: John Peavler
Production artist: Kathy Bergstrem
Photographers: Christine Polomsky and Al Parrish
Stylist: Jan Nickum
PHOTO CREDITS
Sarah Donnelly: photos on pages 1, 2, 6, 12, 16, 124, 125
Cara McClarty: photo on page 3

metric conversion chart

TO CONVERT	TO	MULTIPLY BY
Inches	Centimeters	2.54
Centimeters	Inches	0.4
Feet	Centimeters	30.5
Centimeters	Feet	0.03
Yards	Meters	0.9
Meters	Yards	1.1
Sq. Inches	Sq. Centimeters	6.45
Sq. Centimeters	Sq. Inches	0.16
Sq. Feet	Sq. Meters	0.09
Sq. Meters	Sq. Feet	10.8
Sq. Yards	Sq. Meters	0.8
Sq. Meters	Sq. Yards	1.2
Pounds	Kilograms	0.45
Kilograms	Pounds	2.2
Ounces	Grams	28.4
Grams	Ounces	0.04

Acknowledgments

➤ I am indebted to my guides at North Light Books: Maggie Moschell, my editor, filled with wisdom and wisecracks, and Greg Albert, Christine Polomsky, Sally Ann Finnegan and Julia Groh. One hundred thank-yous!

➤ I am grateful to the Society of Craft Designers and my many colleagues and friends there.

➤ Thank you to the companies and individuals who generously provided materials and information for the projects in this book, including Milestones Products, E-Z Craft Products, Wits End Mosaics, Sea Glass Inc. and Greg Quinn at Salmon Bay Sand & Gravel.

➤ A warm thanks to my local network of friends and colleagues whose never-ending supply of knowledge, encouragement, inspiration and humor saw me through the making of this book: Miriam Works, David George Gordon, Ellie David, Amy Gaffney, Anne Kepple, Duane Cromwell, Bill Anschuetz, Cara McClarty, Lorie Dwinell, Buffalo McGillvray, Patsy Moreland, Steph Mader, Laurie Lile, Karol Campbell, Bob Campbell and Denise Olivier.

➤ My gratitude and appreciation goes out to those not mentioned here who encouraged me the entire way. And to my students — my best teachers, who continue to inspire and surprise me.

About the Author ➤ Sarah Donnelly began experimenting with color and design at a very young age at a kid-size easel in her mother's painting studio. During elementary school, her "handyman" father taught her how to fix things; as Donnelly & Daughter, they embarked on many nearly-disastrous plumbing repair projects. These early childhood experiences proved to be excellent training for Sarah's lifelong willingness to fling herself into untried projects. Since then, she has been breaking things apart and putting them back together, with surprising results.

She has spent many years working in design fields such as graphics production, packaging design, product development for the craft industry and creating functional art pieces for sale through galleries. Sarah currently spends her days making art, teaching mosaic workshops, writing and exhibiting her work in retail galleries and art exhibits in the Pacific Northwest. Her design work, teaching and writing are inevitably imbued with humor and enthusiasm.

Like her early experiments with painting, plumbing, breaking and repairing things, Sarah's mosaic designs are uninhibited, fluid and festive. Most importantly, she has done the experimenting so that the projects in this book will work well for the beginner as well as for the more advanced mosaic artist. Sarah's wish is that this book serve as an entryway to mosaics, supplying information, instruction and inspiration to those who dare to be creative.

table of
contents

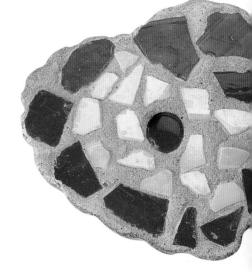

Introduction ➤

You probably cringe at the sound of breaking glass, but it's music to my ears because it means a new mosaic is about to begin. My interest in mosaic-making has grown over many years from a passing fancy to a passionate fascination. When I began exploring mosaic art, I discovered that many mosaics can be complicated and messy to make, requiring large investments in special tools and many hours of patient work. I yearned for a fun, inventive, foolproof method that I could do in one rainy afternoon. So this is how my book of easy mosaic projects came into being!

If you are making your first mosaic, these projects were created with you in mind. If you've already made some mosaics, stay put because as the book progresses, the projects become more challenging and creative. All of the projects are flat and portable: stepping stones, wall plaques, patio tabletops, house signs and garden stakes. Some are useful; others are decorative. The designs are clear, bold and playful. The instructions are detailed but not complicated, and the sequence and nature of the steps stay the same throughout the book.

The materials and tools are common and easy to find. It's hard to go wrong with broken materials such as glass and ceramics. Concrete is truly amazing. It is easy to mold to different shapes and sizes; it anchors a wide variety of mosaic materials; and mistakes are easy to fix. Once you've gathered your supplies, you can do any of these projects in two to three hours. Basic how-to's are covered in detail in the Getting Started section of the book. Individual projects will refer you to specific page numbers for in-depth, step-by-step instructions.

If you know how to bake a cake, you will catch on very quickly. If not, it will take more time—approximately one minute more! In fact, these projects have a lot in common with baking a cake. First, you lay out and organize your mosaic design on paper. Then blend a small amount of concrete mix and water—like cake mix—and empty it into a mold—like a cake pan. Then smooth the surface—like frosting—position a stencil on top, and finally transfer, arrange and push in your mosaic pieces—like adding candles and candy sprinkles. It's a piece of cake!

Although I can't claim sole credit for inventing this method, I have explored it to its limits and have created some wonderful projects for you to try. To make the process as simple as possible, I've eliminated several steps that other mosaic techniques require.

✴ My method does not demand the cutting and nipping of glass pieces. That technique requires special tools, time and patience, and it can be frustrating to master. As you gain experience and confidence you may want to try cutting your own pieces, but even beginners can achieve satisfying results utilizing broken glass or ceramic pieces for every project in this book.

✴ My method provides patterns so you don't have to worry about your drawing skills.

✴ My method utilizes a mold filled with wet stepping stone mix rather than a base onto which mosaic pieces must be glued before they are grouted. Consequently, each project is self-grouting: you simply push pieces directly into the wet mix and you do not have to wait for any glue to dry.

✴ My method is direct: there are no backward images to confuse you. What you see is what you get.

As you advance through the projects in this book, you will learn important concepts and valuable skills, such as how to create a unified design by controlling the space between the pieces and how to balance the contrast between foreground and background. You will discover techniques and ideas that you might want to explore further. As you follow the various steps from start to finish you will become more proficient while you're developing greater patience and flexibility. After you've completed a few projects, I encourage you to experiment. Don't limit yourself to the shapes and sizes described in this book. Think big: make a tabletop. Think small: make a paperweight. Be bold: embed odds and ends directly into the wet mix. Once you get started making these fun and easy mosaics, I predict the sound of breaking glass will become music to your ears, too!

Tools

Most of the tools you will need may be found around the house or garage. The most useful special items to invest in are a couple of unusual molds, specially formulated concrete mix, color pigment and a dust mask.

1 Stepping stone molds and tart pans are some of the molds you can use. Manufactured molds come in a variety of shapes: round, square, hexagon, octagon, butterfly and flower.

2 Milestones Products makes a specially formulated, light-gray concrete called StoneCraft Mix. It has a very smooth texture and is workable for about one hour. It comes in two sizes: 7 and 3½ pounds (3.2 and 6.3kg). A perfectly good alternative is vinyl concrete patcher made by Quikrete and other manufacturers. It follows similar mixing proportions but dries a somewhat darker gray. It is available in 6- and 20-pound (2.7 and 9kg) pails, and in 40-pound (18kg) bags at home improvement stores and lumberyards. It is easier to use one brand of concrete so that you can become accustomed to its properties. Don't combine different brands of dry mix.

3 Powdered pigment for coloring concrete is available at craft stores, potter's supply stores and home improvement centers. Liquid pigment is also available.

4 A dust mask is essential to wear when mixing dry concrete or cleaning up broken glass. I recommend investing in one that is a notch above the cheapest.

5 Rubber gloves protect hands from wet concrete mix and sharp, broken glass and tile.

6 Goggles or eye protection must be worn when breaking glass and during the stone clean-up step.

7 An apron protects your clothes.

8 A rigid board is used for moving a newly-poured stone in a mold.

9 A round-bottomed 18" (46cm) diameter plastic bowl is ideal for mixing concrete. The smaller bowl is used for soaking ceramic tiles.

10 A large measuring cup is used to measure water for making the stepping stone mix.

11 A water spray bottle is needed for misting your stone while it cures.

12 A wooden paddle or garden spade is used for blending concrete and water.

13 A plastic putty knife, wall scraper or even an old credit card may be used for smoothing the surface of the wet concrete mix.

14 Duct tape and corrugated cardboard scraps are used for making an indentation in the back of a stone for hanging.

15 A fine-grain sanding block or sandpaper is used to smooth sharp edges of broken glass and ceramic tile.

16 Ruler

17 Scissors

18 A craft or utility knife and several sharp blades are required for cutting out the patterns to make the Mold Templates.

19 Felt-tip pen

20 A pencil with an eraser is used for moving and embedding tiny mosaic pieces and for making dots in the wet mix.

21 Large tweezers are useful for picking up tiny tesserae.

22 A hammer covered with a sock can be used to break glass. A rubber mallet also works.

23 A hacksaw is used for one project to cut a terra-cotta pot.

24 Plastic bags are used for containing breaking glass and covering wet concrete.

25 Rags or a towel

26 A foam paintbrush or sponge is used to clean mosaic pieces and smooth the wet concrete surface.

27 A paper clip is used for cleaning hardened concrete from the mosaic pieces.

28 A screwdriver is used to scrape the edges of the hardened stone.

29 Transparent vinyl contact paper may be used for saving and transferring mosaic layouts.

30 A tray of fine sand may be used for laying out pebble and rock mosaic designs.

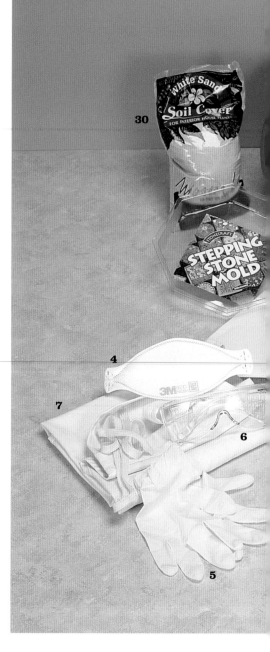

31 A small paintbrush and dishwashing liquid, petroleum jelly or cooking oil spray are used for coating molds which might otherwise adhere to the concrete. Commercial release agents are also available at home improvement stores.

32 A 5-gallon (3.8l) bucket with water is used for rinsing wet concrete mix from your tools and bowl so you won't clog your sink drain.

33 Paper is used for tracing the mold when you are doing a project that does not use a photocopied pattern.

34 An awl is used to punch holes through a paper pattern for transferring leaf stems and other linear design elements to the wet mix.

35 A toothbrush, scouring pad and sponge are used fto clean hardened mix from the mosaic pieces after the stone has cured.

Tesserae

Tesserae are the pieces which make up your mosaic design. You should be familiar with the characteristics of various types of tesserae because some materials are better for certain uses. For example, mosaics made of porous materials are more susceptible to cracking in cold weather. Keep these features in mind when considering the design, use and location of your mosaic creation.

Glass

✻ **Vitreous glass** tiles, also known as Venetian tesserae, come in uniform sizes and are very versatile. The opaque tiles are smooth on one side and ridged on the other for better bonding. Practical and economical, they are strong, non-porous, and stain- and weather-resistant. The color selection is good and they are easy to break or cut. Buy them loose or on 12" x 12" (30cm x 30cm) sheets.

✻ **Stained glass** or art glass has both smooth and textured surfaces with irregularities: bubbles, swirls and waves. The opaque glass is more practical for mosaic purposes because the gray concrete will not show through. Since this glass is very thin, it must be fully embedded in the mix in order to remain in place. Most packaged broken glass has been tumbled to dull the sharp edges.

✻ **Smalti,** or Byzantine tesserae, are made in Italy specifically for mosaic applications. Large, hand-poured glass slabs are hand-cut into small irregular cubes. The surfaces are highly reflective, faceted and pitted, making them semiporous. Smalti come in an amazing selection of intense opaque and transparent colors as well as reflective metallic gold. Since it takes practice to make accurate cuts, it's better to use the cubes whole. They are beautiful and expensive.

✻ **Tumbled glass** is shiny glass that has been machine smoothed so it becomes matte or frosted. This process also breaks the pieces into sizes that are just right for the projects in this book. (If the pieces are large, the chance of fractures increases.) Most "sea glass" is actually broken recycled bottles that have been tumbled.

✻ **Glass nuggets** look like half-melted marbles, flat on one side, rounded on the other. They come in several sizes and many colors. They are used in this book for eyes, grapes, raspberries and other round accents.

✻ **A broken mirror** isn't bad luck for a mosaic artist, because just a few pieces can add a lot of sparkle to any mosaic design. Before using, seal the reverse side with two light coats of acrylic spray or other sealant to prevent the silvering from deteriorating when it comes in contact with the caustic wet concrete.

Broken china and pottery

Save those chipped bowls and shattered plates! You can embed an entire broken plate or use pieces of patterned china as accents. I recommend sanding the sharp edges, especially if you're using the pieces in a stepping stone.

Ceramic tile

Ceramic tile is available in many different finishes, from rough and rustic to highly polished. Ceramic tiles are produced in uniform sizes and shapes and are inexpensive. Buy them loose or on sheets. Tile is easily cut with nippers or broken with a hammer. Some types of tiles to try in your mosaic designs are:

✻ **Glazed floor** and wall tile has a thin highly reflective glaze on one side. It may be porous and isn't reversible.

✻ **Unglazed tile** has a nonreflective matte finish and is reversible. It's strong, easy to cut and may be porous.

✻ **Porcelain** is high-fired ceramic that comes glazed and unglazed. It's the least porous and toughest of all tiles and is usually waterproof and weather-resistant.

Stones and shells

Pebbles, shells and rock (such as granite and marble) are manufactured by Mother Nature to be irregular, imperfect and unique. There is a wide variety of shapes, sizes and finishes: from natural matte to highly polished. They are available in a beautiful but limited natural color range or are coated with bright paint or clear acrylic. Hard stones are very durable and resistant to water and weather. Manufactured stone tiles and cubes of marble are easy to break but difficult to cut.

Found objects

"Junque" is cheap, free and fun. You can use broken bottles, keys, buttons, beads, trinkets and brass charms — almost anything not made of plastic or rubber (which don't adhere to concrete). Sort through your drawers for unique items and have fun experimenting!

1 translucent stained glass	**15** mirror tiles	**29** toys
2 opaque stained glass	**16** glazed ceramic wall and floor tiles	**30** drawer pull
3 stained glass with iridized surface	**17** unglazed earthenware tiles	**31** spoon
4 translucent smalti	**18** decorative porcelain tiles	**32** assorted found objects
5 opaque smalti	**19** china and pottery	**33** broken chandelier crystal
6 gold smalti	**20** polished and unpolished river rocks	**34** metal house numbers
7 glass nuggets	**21** painted gravel	**35** terra-cotta frog
8 vitreous glass tiles	**22** white marble	**36** alphabet press set
9 pressed glass star	**23** granite	**37** decorative scrolls and border stamps
10 beach glass or sea glass	**24** seashells	**38** oversized rubber stamp
11 chunky glass, tumbled	**25** keys	**39** cookie cutters
12 glass rods	**26** coins	**40** craft stick
13 glass beads	**27** costume jewelry	
14 fused-glass heart ornament	**28** buttons	

Crazy Paving

The layout of the individual pieces of a mosaic give the design its energy. Many mosaics are made up of a simple, repetitious pattern. Imagine a brick wall, row upon row of rectangular bricks all evenly spaced. This is a predictable and calm pattern. Other familiar patterns include circles, overlapping fans, basket weave, and herringbone, which are graceful and have more motion and fluidity than the wall. Every mosaicist learns that the **joint**, the mortar-filled space between the bricks, is just as important as the bricks themselves. These spaces move your eyes in a desired direction and rhythm.

The projects in this book use only one pattern: **crazy paving,** also known as **opus palladianum,** which is a busy arrangement of broken, irregularly shaped pieces of glass, ceramic and stone. What sets it apart from other more traditional patterns is its broken lines, unpredictable fractures, and its seeming chaos. It is a high-energy, fun, and sometimes dizzying pattern.

Crazy paving is extremely versatile. It easily lends itself to portraying a variety of forms. The designs in this book are simple, bold shapes that when expressed as a crazy-pave mosaic will remain interesting and easy to recognize. Each design is unique, yet repeatable many times over. No two crazy-pave mosaics will ever look the same due to the unique arrangement of broken shards and pieces.

Most of these designs consist of a crazy-paved shape within a plain gray background. The image stands out clearly against the unadorned concrete. The background and foreground aren't competing for attention so the eye has an easier time "reading" the image.

Crazy paving is the perfect mosaic pattern for beginners. The irregular arrangement of tesserae allows for inconsistencies but it is fun and challenging for the more experienced mosaicist. Laying out a design is quick and easy because it is less complicated and intricate than other paving patterns. The technique is easy to learn because less time is spent on precision and detail.

Molds

In the following projects, you will cast a concrete stone by filling a shallow mold with thick wet concrete, adding your mosaic pieces and leaving it to harden. There are three kinds of molds: manufactured, makeshift, and made-from-scratch. Craft stores carry a variety of shapes and sizes of molds that are specifically designed for casting stones. Some molds are flexible vinyl which can last through many castings. Others are more expensive heavy-duty, rigid plastic which can be used almost indefinitely.

When hunting for makeshift molds, you should consider the material and the angle of the sides. The material I prefer is flexible plastic because it releases hardened concrete very easily and it's reusable. Molds can also be made of rigid plastic, wood, plaster, or corrugated cardboard (which must be coated with a thin layer of release agent). Spray cans of mold release are sold at home improvement centers or you can use dishwashing liquid, cooking oil spray or petroleum jelly. You can also line these molds with heavy plastic sheeting or garbage bags, but any wrinkles in the plastic will show up on your stone.

A makeshift mold is a container that came into this world intended for another use. For example, assorted sizes of round, vinyl plant saucers can be used as molds for mosaic stones of various sizes. If you want to make a five-paver garden path, you can buy five inexpensive plant saucers and mold your stones all at once. We buy and throw away potential molds every day. Blister display packaging is made of plastic that wet concrete easily forms to and hardened concrete easily releases from. Many food products are protected or served in plastic containers which serve as perfect casting molds: deli and bakery containers, microwave food trays, margarine tubs, party trays and lids. Other unusual plastic mold substitutes are soap and candle molds, dog food bowls, garbage can lids and plant flats lined with plastic.

You should look for containers with sides that angle outward. Even if you coat a straight-sided metal with mold release, your hardened stone may not come out. However, your stone will pop right out of a coated metal pie pan that has angled sides.

Here are a few suggestions for non-plastic molds: metal pie pans, tart and springform pans; waxed paper cups and foil roasting pans. A cardboard pizza box without a plastic liner makes a rustic-looking stone: just fill it with concrete mix, push in your mosaic pieces, let it harden, then tear off the box. Any embedded cardboard fragments will disintegrate when exposed to the elements.

If you're handy with tools, you may want to make your own molds "from scratch." Build a plywood frame or make a freeform shape with a flexible garden border and stakes shoved into the ground; pack wet sand into a cardboard box and carve out a shape; or simply dig a shallow hole in the dirt and empty your wet concrete mix into it.

If you have a choice, it's best to select molds that have smooth bottoms. This will allow you to try the indirect method of creating a mosaic. Instead of filling the mold with wet mix and placing the tesserae on the top surface (the direct method that's described in this book), the bottom of the mold is lined with contact paper, sticky side up. Tesserae are arranged on the contact paper with the design reversed. Then wet mix, usually fast-setting concrete, is poured into the mold. When the stone is hard, it is removed from the mold and the contact paper is peeled off to reveal the design. This method creates a mosaic with a smooth, shiny top surface. Although the instructions in this book are for the direct method, you may use the designs in this book with either method.

In the project instructions "prepare the mold" means for you to apply mold release if needed, or attach the wall mount to the bottom of the mold (more about this later), or rinse out a previously used mold. A clean mold will release a stone smoothly and easily.

tip

1. Beveled sides are a must.

2. Flexible plastic and rubber molds do not need mold release.

3. Metal and rigid plastic molds require a coat of mold release.

Smashing Technique

What is the purpose of breaking perfectly good, usable bowls, tiles, plates and sheets of glass? It's fun and it's a good excuse to make a truly unique mosaic. Look for old china and tile at flea markets, secondhand stores and yard sales. Look around your house for cracked or chipped china that may be more useful smashed to create a mosaic design.

A hammer is the perfect tool for pounding in nails, but it's too dense and

MATERIALS

safety glasses

rubber gloves

dust mask

plate to be broken

rubber mallet or hammer covered with old socks fastened with rubber bands

old towel

heavyweight transparent plastic bag

pointed for glass-smashing purposes. The hardened steel head shatters the glass or china in one place, sending straight cracks radiating in all directions. The result is often pointed, elongated and very sharp shards. Fine china may even turn into dust when hit with a claw hammer.

A rubber mallet is a perfect smashing tool because it will break glass just as easily as a hammer, but the pieces will be more irregular and interesting in size and shape. If you don't have a rubber mallet handy, you can wrap a hammer head with one or two old socks and use a rubber band to hold them on.

Smash on a surface you do not value, preferably the newspaper-padded concrete floor of your garage or basement. If you want to smash plates in your kitchen, protect the floor with a piece of plywood or a thick towel. And while we're talking

about protection, don't forget to protect your eyes from airborne glass shards.

How hard you must hit the glass to break it depends on the type of glass. Bone china will be easier to break than stoneware or ceramic bathroom tile. Sometimes an object will break perfectly and completely with one stroke. Other times it may refuse to break after five or ten whacks, and you hesitate to hit it any harder lest you smash it to smithereens. Try propping the stubborn piece against a brick or another piece of broken pottery; it will more readily break into usable pieces.

If you want to break a tile or plate and reassemble it "whole" in your mosaic design, apply strips of strong tape to one side before you smash it.

1 ➤ **Wrap.** Put on goggles and gloves. Center the plate on the towel, then wrap it up.

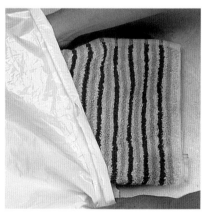

2 ➤ **Ready.** Place the towel in the plastic bag and fold the open end under, sealing the bag.

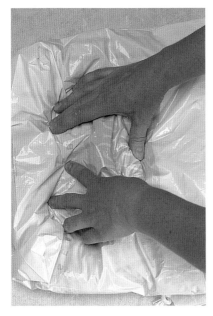

3 ➤ Aim. Check for the placement of the plate in the bag.

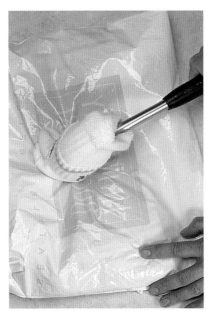

4 ➤ Smash! Take one light swing at it. Peek in the bag to see what kind of damage you did. Handle sharp pieces with gloved hands and extreme care.

5 ➤ Voilà! Broken bits! It may take two or more blows to break the plate into usable pieces, about 2"x 2" (5cm x 5cm) and smaller.

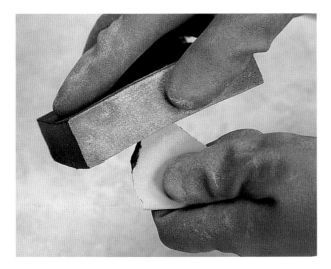

6 ➤ Sand off the sharp edges. You may use the pieces as they are or, to make them safer and easier to work with, you may want to sand down all of the edges. This is time-consuming, but a good idea. If you plan to walk on your stepping stone barefoot, you will definitely want to blunt the edges because some will be exposed in the finished mosaic.

Put on the dust mask and safety glasses when you sweep up broken leftovers. Fine particles of glass and clay will be airborne and undetectable.

tip

Save any leftover broken bits in glass jars. They will be easy to identify, safe to handle and beautiful to see.

Planning Your Mosaic

Here are some things to consider when you design and gather the materials for your mosaic:

Will the stone be functional or decorative?

Do you want to hang it on a wall?

Will it be indoors or outdoors? Will it be exposed to weather extremes or in a protected area? Would it be convenient to remove it and bring it indoors during freezing weather?

Do you want to leave space to write a name or date, or make a hand print?

Is it part of a series (a path, for example) or does it stand on its own?

What colors of tesserae and concrete do you want?

These and other points will be covered as we go. Look through the projects and choose one you like. If this is your first mosaic, consider trying one of the simpler designs: the apple, pear, bananas, mirrored heart, river rock path or the maple leaf. Buy or find a mold in a size and shape you like.

It's important to choose colors that you like. Craft stores carry mosaic pieces in a variety of shapes, sizes and colors. If you are unable to find the exact color of mosaic pieces shown in a photograph, you'll need to improvise. You may have a chipped plate in the perfect color that you don't mind sacrificing to make your work of art. A store that sells stained glass may have just what you're looking for, and you can usually buy a small portion of a large sheet which will break into more than enough pieces for your project. Boxes of small pieces of scrap glass are often available at reduced prices. The Internet also offers easy access to the world of mosaic materials. Estimate what you'll need, then buy a little more just to be safe. Going back later to match a ceramic or glass color is difficult or impossible.

The red in this simple border design contrasts beautifully with the green foliage that surrounds the plaque.

Making the Templates

Templates are your guide to laying out your mosaic design. Most of the projects in this book call for two templates: a Design Template and a Mold Template.

The Design Template is for your initial layout of tesserae. It's where you arrange the pieces that will create your mosaic design. Use the template to practice outlining shapes, to experiment with spacing and to make your final arrangement of pieces.

The Mold Template determines the position of your design within the edges of the mold. After the mix has been poured into the mold and smoothed, this template is placed on the surface of the wet mix. The cut-out shape makes a window which you use for transferring and positioning all the mosaic pieces in your design.

1 ➤ Enlarge the pattern. All of the patterns in this book have been reduced in size. Use a copier to enlarge the pattern to fit your mold, using 11" x 17" (28cm x 43cm) paper if possible. Bring your mold or a tracing of it with you to the copy machine so you can check the fit of the enlarged pattern. Try to keep the outlines of the pattern ⅜" (1cm) but no closer than ¼" (6mm) from the edges of the mold. You may have to experiment with different percentages to get the right size. The advantage of this technique is that you can use the patterns in this book with molds of many shapes and sizes. When the enlargement is correct, make a second copy.

2 ➤ Position the mold and trace it. Set your mold base-side down on the enlarged pattern over the design. This will be easier if you have a clear plastic mold and can see the pattern through the mold. Check to see that the design outline is ⅜" (1cm) from the edge of the mold, and trace around the base of the mold. It's OK if the mold runs off the edge of the paper copy. You need only a partial mold outline to properly position the template on the mix surface. Use scissors to cut along the mold outline.

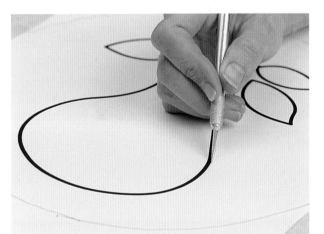

3 ➤ Cut out the design. Use a craft knife or small scissors to cut out the design outline. Cut on the outside of the line, making as large an opening as possible. You can lift out the design shapes and use them for your Design Template if you didn't make two copies of your pattern initially. The template with the cut-out areas is your Mold Template, which is the one you will place on the wet mix surface when you're ready to transfer your tesserae.

Using the Design Template

Before you lay out your design, it is helpful to organize your tesserae in trays or shoe box lids, using one tray per color. For some designs, sorting pieces by size and shape is also a good idea. A white-lined tray for translucent glass shows truer colors, although a gray background shows how the glass will look when placed on the concrete.

If you lay out your mosaic in the following order, you will save some time and reduce your frustration. Start by finding and placing key mosaic pieces: points, corners, narrow bands, and tight spaces. Next, outline the shape. Finally, fill in the rest of the shape.

When you have your colors organized, begin to arrange the mosaic pieces on the Design Template. Practice putting pieces together like a jigsaw puzzle, leaving ⅛" (3mm) between the pieces. For some people, this step will take great patience. However, for many of us, this is a relaxing, creative, engrossing activity. Take your time and keep in mind that when you transfer the pieces to the surface of the wet mix, their positions will change slightly. Don't worry, you will have the chance to fine-tune the placement of the pieces before you embed them.

MATERIALS

Design Template

tesserae

trays to hold and sort mosaic pieces

1 ➤ Select the key pieces. Tesserae come in many shapes, but generally broken glass or ceramic pieces have straight, gently curved, and angular edges. Your eyes will learn to pick out certain shapes and curves. Key pieces such as points should be selected and positioned first.

2 ➤ Position the key pieces. Try to break down each design into several smaller shapes or parts. Then find key pieces to highlight and define each shape. For example, triangular pieces are perfect for pointed leaf tips, feathers, beaks, toes, animal ears, bent knee joints and tight corners on numerals.

tip

Lay out translucent tesserae on concrete-gray colored paper for a realistic preview.

3 ➤ Select round shapes. Experiment with various round shapes for eyes or spots: glass beads, buttons, glass nuggets, marbles or thumbtacks. Avoid plastic beads and items made of rubber, which do not adhere to the concrete.

4 ➤ Outline the shapes. The outlines of your design include all kinds of bends and twists. Making a good outline is especially critical because we are using the crazy pave pattern. The outline needs to be bold and clean to organize the fractured and busy pattern of lines within. Simple shapes with smooth outlines are usually the most effective.

Some curves are long and gradual.

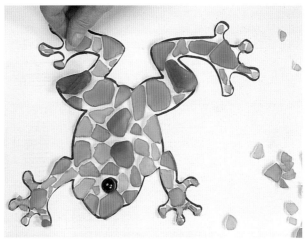

Others are short with tight bends. Try to match the curve of the line as best as you can because you may see it clearly now, but when you take away the paper template, it may look very different. Your placement of pieces has to re-create that line as closely as possible so that anyone can easily "read" the image.

Using the Design Template
> continued

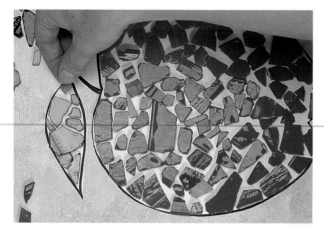

5 ➤ Fill in the middle. As you fill in the shape, pay attention to the spaces between the pieces, which are called **joints**. Spacing affects the "readability" of an image because the design is created by broken pieces. The closer the spacing of the pieces, the easier it is to see the image as a unified whole. Larger spacing between the pieces emphasizes the shapes of the individual pieces, making it more difficult to see the image as a single shape. However, don't space the pieces too closely; allow enough space for the wet mix to come up and anchor each individual tessera. Generally, I try to allow ⅛" (3mm) between pieces.

6 ➤ Adjust the spacing. The shape of the tesserae affects the spacing. Flat tesserae should be spaced evenly thoughout a design.

Round or irregularly-shaped tesserae such as rocks or glass nuggets are difficult to space evenly. The rocks may look fine on the paper template, but when the pieces are partially submerged in the mix, they will shrink and the joints between them will widen. The image will not "read" very well. To solve this problem, rocks, nuggets and other rounded tesserae should be placed so they touch each other. Lay out rounded tesserae in a box of sand so that you can see how they'll appear after they are embedded.

Preparing the Mold with a Mounting Device

If you are planning to make a stone that will hang (on a wall, fence, or door) complete these steps before preparing the mix. This is an inexpensive way to create a rectangular indentation in the back of your stone to accommodate one or more nails or screws. The indentation should be ¼" to ⅜" (6mm-9mm) deep and wide enough for two nails or screws, since a 12" (30cm) stone weighs over 7 pounds (3.2kg) and may require heavy-duty screws set in anchors in your wall. When you hang your stone you will be able to adjust the plaque from side to side to center and straighten it. Any project may be turned into a wall plaque by adding this mounting device.

MATERIALS

2" x 2" (5cm x 5cm) piece of corrugated cardboard

3" x 2" (8cm x 5cm) piece of duct tape

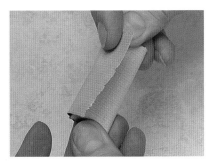

1 ➤ Bend the cardboard. Set the mold on a rigid board. Bend the piece of cardboard in half.

2 ➤ Wrap the cardboard with tape. Wrap the folded cardboard with the piece of duct tape sticky-side out.

3 ➤ Secure the ends of the tape. Overlap the ends of the tape so it sticks to itself and flattens the bent cardboard piece. The sticky cardboard mounting device should now be about 2" x 1" x ¼" (5cm x 2.5cm x 6mm) and ready to position.

4 ➤ Position the mounting device. Place the mounting device centered in your mold, about 1½" (38mm) from the top edge.

When you unmold your stone, the tape will stick to the mold and you will have to peel it away as your stone releases. Use a stick or screwdriver to remove the cardboard and duct tape from the stone. The stone will have a depression to accommodate two screws or nails for hanging the plaque.

tip

Use the plastic hanging tab of the mold as a marker for the top of a round or square stone. If there is no tab, stick a small piece of tape on the edge to mark the top. When you place your tesserae, you'll know which edge is the top of your wall plaque.

Concrete

Concrete is an amazing material. It can be formed into just about any shape: a plain concrete block, a sidewalk, a park bench, garden statuary, foundation walls, bridge footings or even skyscrapers. All of these objects begin as a soft, malleable mixture which is placed in a mold. Within a short time the mixture hardens into a strong and durable material: concrete. It used to be considered a building material only. Now it's being used everywhere, outdoors and indoors, as a functional and decorative surface for kitchen counters, bathroom floors, front door columns; and for this book, wall plaques, house signs, tabletops, garden stakes, paperweights and stepping stones.

First, I want to discuss terminology. Is it cement or concrete? Cement, concrete, grout, mix and mortar are often used interchangeably to refer to the material used to fill in around tesserae, but in fact they refer to different types of mixtures. Each was created for a specific purpose, but they all have one thing in common: each contains cement, a very fine powder of crushed rocks. I learned to keep the terms straight by remembering that

cement is to concrete (and all the others) what flour is to a cake. It's an ingredient.

The projects in this book use **concrete** or **mix** that is specially formulated for making smooth-textured, long-lasting, gray stepping stones. It also works for making other objects, as you will see. It comes in convenient 3½- and 7-pound (1.6kg and 3.2kg) bags, a very manageable size and quantity compared to the large and heavy bags of concrete mix sold at home improvement centers. Stepping stone mix is sold at craft stores and garden centers. Most concrete is gray, but white is also available and colorant may be added to make any other desired color.

Mixing concrete is an inexact science, but it is very easy to do. It is a forgiving medium with very few absolutes; most mistakes can easily be corrected. And it's less messy than you may think, so don't be afraid to experiment and have fun!

Some conditions which influence the strength and durability of concrete are the amount of water used in the mix, temperature and humidity, and the hardening or **curing** conditions. Concrete should last

for a very long time when mixed in ideal circumstances: moderate temperature, no direct sun or high wind, mixed with as little water as possible, and kept moist while hardening. Use my measurements as a starting point; no two mixtures will ever be the same. As you make more stones, you'll develop a feel for the conditions that affect the mix on any given day.

If you are not using a premeasured bag of mix, estimate the amount of dry mix you will need by measureing the amount of water it takes to fill the mold. You will need roughly the same amount of dry mix, but add an extra cup just to be safe. For every 5 cups (1.6kg) of dry mix, start with 1 cup (236ml) of water. Different manufacturers' proportions may vary.

Your workspace can be in your kitchen or garage on a level surface at a comfortable height for working. (Although you may want to prepare the mix outdoors.) Protect the work surface with plastic or newspaper, put on an apron and gather your tools and materials for the next step: preparing the mix.

Here are two molds with the correct amount of dry mix needed for each. The packets at the bottom of the photo are powdered pigments that can be added to color the concrete.

Preparing the Mix

When you are told to "prepare the mix" in the instructions for the projects, keep in mind the Tips (below) and follow the steps on pages 24-26.

MATERIALS

dust mask

rubber gloves

one bag of dry stepping stone mix

scissors

mixing bowl

measuring cup

teaspoon

water

mixing tool, garden trowel or spade

mold

rigid board 16" x 16" (41cm x 41cm)

smoothing tool: 3" (75mm) plastic putty knife or trowel

5-gallon (3.8l) bucket half filled with water to clean tools

optional: one-hour timer

tips

➤ Always wear a dust mask and rubber gloves when mixing concrete.

➤ The less water used initially, the stronger the final stone. Start with less water than called for, especially if you have only one small bag of mix.

➤ Use drinkable water only; impurities may weaken the stone.

➤ Use mix specifically formulated for stepping stones, or an equivalent product. Do not use generic concrete mixes, which usually contain coarse gravel. Do not use fast-setting concrete.

➤ Measured amounts are approximate; use them as a starting point. Have extra dry mix on hand to make adjustments.

➤ Prepare you mix in a temperate location: 55-75°F (13-24°C).

➤ Use a mold material which allows the hardened stone to release easily: rubber or flexible plastic

➤ Other mold materials (metals, cardboard, rigid plastic or wood) may need to be coated with a release agent. Use a commercially available release agent, dishwashing liquid, cooking oil spray or petroleum jelly.

➤ Do not use straight-sided pans. Use molds with sides which are angled outward, even slightly.

➤ Use a rigid board to lift a flexible mold once it has been filled with wet mix to avoid creating an unseen crack.

➤ The fewer and shallower the impressions you make in the stone (writing, stamping, mounting device, etc.), the stronger it will be.

➤ Do not embed any more pieces after the stone begins to harden or set up, about one hour after adding water. If the surface cracks, spray it once with water, smooth it, and set it aside to harden.

➤ Allow the molded stone to harden at a moderate temperature and in a level, undisturbed place away from sunlight.

➤ Spray the curing stone liberally with water daily for the first seven days.

➤ Wait 48 hours before removing your stone from the mold.

➤ Wait at least fourteen days before stepping on a stone.

➤ Do not put concrete or mix down any drains; it may harden and clog the pipes. Instead, rinse your bowl and tools in a bucket of water. Let the water settle overnight, drain off the clear water into your yard and dispose of the gray concrete sludge in the garbage.

➤ Store concrete mix in a dry place in an airtight container or plastic bag.

Preparing the Mix
> continued

3 ➤ Mix well. Using the mixing tool, thoroughly combine the dry mix with the water. This photo shows a desirable consistency. The mixture looks coarse and a little crumbly.

1 ➤ Empty the dry mix into a bowl. Try to mix concrete outdoors whenever possible. Put on a dust mask and gloves. Cut open the bag of mix and gently pour it into the mixing bowl. Keep the dust to a minimum by pouring and mixing slowly. If you want to color your mix, turn to page 27 for directions.

2 ➤ Add water. Add exactly 2 cups (472ml) of water, a few teaspoons (5-10ml) less if you are in a humid or damp climate (follow the manufacturer's instructions if the amount given is different from this).

The amount of water added to the dry mix determines the durability and strength of the finished stone. **Use the least amount of water possible to reach a workable consistency.** This amount will vary with the brand of mix you're using, the air and water temperatures, and the humidity. If the mixture is so thin that it can be poured, it will make a weaker, less durable stone. A wet, sloppy mix will delay hardening and will be too watery to hold embedded objects. If the mixture is too dry, it will be hard to work with, but this is easy to correct. It's best to begin with a mixture that appears to be a bit too dry.

4 ➤ Test the consistency. Pick up a handful in your gloved hand and press together firmly. Does it stay in one lump without any cracks or crumbling? If so, it's mixed correctly. Go to Step 5. If it crumbles easily when poked, add more water.

TOO DRY!
This mixture needs just a little more water.
Trust me: 1 teaspoon (5ml) of water will go a
long way, especially when you are about to
reach the "just right" point. Blend very well
and test again before adding another tea-
spoonful. If it's a hot day, you may need more
water, but add just a little at a time.

TOO WET!
This mixture is soupy, runny and unusable.
You should add a small amount of dry mix
and stir well. Keep adding and stirring until
your mixture is "just right."

JUST RIGHT!
If you've mixed it correctly, the mix should
hold together in your hand—and in the
bowl—in one lump or mass. It should be fairly
smooth and plastic, like thick cookie batter.

**5 ➤ Empty the mixture into
the mold.** Put your mold on a
rigid board and empty the mix
into the mold, which should "plop"
into the mold in one lump. Remove
your mask and check the time.
You have about 45 to 60 minutes,
weather and temperature permit-
ting—usually plenty of time to
finish a project. If it's dry and hot,
you may have only 45 minutes. If
it's wet and cool, you'll have more
time to work. I like to set a timer
for 35 minutes, so when it rings I
know I have ten or twenty minutes
left before the mix starts to harden.

6 ➤ Spread out the mix.
Use your mixing tool to quickly
and rather unevenly spread out
the mix in the mold, especially
into the corners and rippled edges
if your mold has them. You'll have
a chance to level the surface in
Step 8.

Preparing the Mix
> continued

7 ➤ Smooth and compact the mix. Now use the putty knife to tamp down the mix and smooth the surface. Go over it several times, turning the mold to get the tool into the corners if your mold has them. Last, smooth the entire edge.

8 ➤ Jiggle the mold. Hold opposite sides of the mold and move the mold one or two inches (25-50mm) back and forth, three or four times in a continuous motion. Rotate the mold 45° and do it again. Rotate and repeat once more. Notice how the mix unifies and the surface smooths out. Jiggle the mold as little as possible, only until the surface is level and the texture evens out. If you jiggle it too much, the mix will start to separate; finer particles will rise to the top, and water will pool on the surface. Don't worry about popping all the bubbles that will arise and don't try to make a perfectly smooth surface now; it will get lumpy when you push in the mosaic pieces. You'll have the chance to smooth it again after embedding your tesserae.

9 ➤ Clean your tools. Rinse out the bowl and tools in a large bucket (never in a sink; see Tips on page 23). Now you have three choices: practice embedding some tesserae; practice incising lines; or put your Mold Template on the mix surface and start transferring tesserae for your first project.

The lime in concrete is caustic and will dry out your skin. It may help to rinse your hands with vinegar to restore the pH balance.

tip

An advantage to this direct, self-grouting technique is that changes can be made and mistakes fixed midway through the project. If you don't like something, remove it, smooth it over and start again. If this is your first stone, take just a couple of minutes after preparing the mix to practice embedding mosaic pieces (see pages 29-30). Try different materials: pieces of glass and tile, a couple of pebbles, a curved piece of a broken cup. Make a line or letter with a craft stick or your finger (see pages 36-37); make a hand print. Then remove all the bits, rinse them off in the bucket of water, smooth the surface and start on your chosen project.

Adding Colorant

Changing a gray stone to a different color is really fun and exciting. It will dramatically affect the look, readability and unity of your mosaic design. The color of the concrete can be changed by adding dry or liquid colorants. Here, I use a packet of powdered pigment. A little goes a long way, so read the instructions carefully. The color of the pigment is much more intense and concentrated than the finished, mixed color. Not all pigments are made for coloring concrete, so be sure to check the manufacturer's instructions. Go for good quality, and match brands with your specific concrete mix. Colorants are available at home improvement centers and most tile and potter's supply stores.

1 ➤ **Add pigment to the dry mix.** Wearing your dust mask and gloves, slowly add the dry colorant to the dry mix before you add water. The powder is **very** messy; it spreads everywhere if touched, and it may stain your clothes.

2 ➤ **Stir.** Slowly stir the two powders together. The mixture may look just as gray as it did before you added the colorant, but don't add more pigment.

Go to page 24 Step 2 for mixing directions. The color develops after water is added, and it will appear darker than the finished stone will look. As the stone cures, the color will lighten.

tip

Lay out tesserae on colored paper that matches your concrete color: gray, terra-cotta, sandstone, light blue or whatever color you have chosen. Experiment to see how the different concrete colors can change the overall look and readability of your design.

Transferring Mosaic Pieces to the Wet Mix

Using a Mold Template

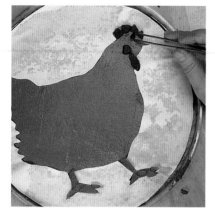

1 ➤ Place the Mold Template. Position the Mold Template on the wet mix surface so that it is flat and smooth. Adjust the location of the design outline within the frame of the mold.

2 ➤ Transfer key pieces. Start transferring pieces to the mix surface, but don't push them in yet. First, the key pieces: points, tips, angles and tight corners.

3 ➤ Outline the figure. Next, transfer the pieces that outline the design. Follow the outline carefully, but work quickly; you can fine-tune the positions in a few minutes.

4 ➤ Fill in the center. Fill in the figure rather quickly. Once all the pieces are moved to the mix, you can adjust the positioning or add more pieces. Keep the pieces inside the cut edge of the Mold Template so you can remove it without disturbing your layout.

When the pieces are in place, step back and look at the arrangement. Is the outline smooth? Is the spacing consistent and close? Make any final adjustments using tweezers to move the pieces. Next you'll embed them.

Transferring with no Template

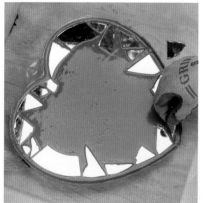

1 ➤ Outline, then fill in. If your design is abstract and covers the entire surface, you won't need a Mold Template. Transfer the border pieces from the Design Template; then fill in the center. If you have several large pieces, or pieces which must be placed precisely, position them first before placing the border pieces.

MATERIALS

Mold Template, cut out
final mosaic layout on Design Template
prepared mix in mold
tesserae
rubber gloves

Embedding Mosaic Pieces

You may begin embedding pieces before or after you remove the Mold Template. If you leave the template in place, it serves as a clear guide for the outline. If you take it off, it's easier to see how the image as a whole "reads," and where changes may be needed. You can decide what to do. The template is reusable if you wipe it off and lay it flat to dry.

The sequence of embedding tesserae is usually determined by the design and the materials. If the design includes an outline, a border around the mold or key pieces, embed them first. As you push them straight down into the mix, be care-ful that these pieces do not shift position. If interior pieces move. you may adjust them. Be sure that each piece of an out-line flows into the next, creating a smooth, even line.

The next priority of the embedding order depends on the thickness of the pieces. If the pieces are of varying thick-ness, embed the thickest piece, followed by thinner and thinner pieces. (Very thin, flat pieces such as coins or bicycle gears and sprockets need to be pushed in more deeply than other pieces to ensure proper bonding and stability.) If pieces are of equal thickness and the design has no important outlines, you may embed them in any sequence.

No matter what order you press in the pieces, you will have to go over all the pieces several times because as you shove one piece into the wet mix another will undoubtedly pop up.

MATERIALS

rubber gloves

pencil with eraser

tweezers

water spray bottle

prepared mix in mold with tesserae on the surface

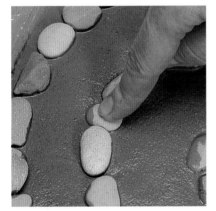

To embed, push straight down at the center of a piece. If it's a flat piece of glass or tile, press until it is flush with the surface of the mix. You want to force the mix to rise up and surround each piece, filling in all the joints without covering the piece. If the piece is pushed in too far, it may sink and disappear or create a crater-like depression (see page 43). If it isn't pushed in enough, it may fall out after the stone has hardened. If a piece is tilted, it will have exposed edges (sharp or not) which can get caught and pop out easily. Overall, it's better to embed pieces a little too deeply rather than not deeply enough.

When you have especially tiny pieces to push in, put the eraser head of a pencil on the piece and push it straight down. A pencil or tweezers may be helpful for moving pieces around and fine-tuning their positions.

If your mosaic piece is rounded, three-dimensional or just unusual (rocks, broken cups, jewelry), it needs to be embedded at least two-thirds of the way in. This is to ensure that the mix comes up and surrounds it so it will stay firmly embedded.

Although I am not wearing them in these photographs, I recommend wearing rubber gloves while embedding to keep the mix from drying out your skin.

Embedding Mosaic Pieces
> continued

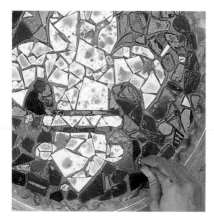

The Law of Mosaic Embedding says, "What goes down must come up (and vice versa)." When you push a mosaic piece down, the mix must come up somewhere else; when you do this to many pieces, the surface will get rough and wavy. This does not mean that you can't make a level, even surface that is good enough to walk on. You can! It just will take some practice. If the surface is a bit uneven, I like to think of it as rippled, textured and much more interesting.

The mosaic material affects the embedding process. Glass, metal, nonporous materials and pieces with straight edges embed very nicely. More difficult to embed are many types of ceramics and rocks because they are porous. When you push them into the wet mix they absorb water from the mix. The surrounding concrete sinks with the piece as you push down, creating a depression. To minimize this effect, soak tile and ceramic pieces in water before embedding. Submerge them until the bubbles stop rising. You can soak them all at once, then do your layout, or soak each piece as you go. Be sure to wipe excess water from the piece before embedding; otherwise the tiny puddle may leave a white powdery stain on the surface that is not desirable and not easy to remove.

Often it can be surprisingly difficult to push certain objects into the mix. Large pebbles, thick hardware and large pieces of tile are the most difficult to embed. Gently seesaw the piece as you're pushing down on it and tap or vibrate it as you push it into the mix. Always embed the thickest pieces first.

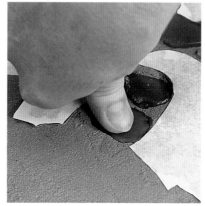

When the mix starts to set up or harden, the pieces will become very difficult to push in. That is your signal to quickly finish embedding the pieces.

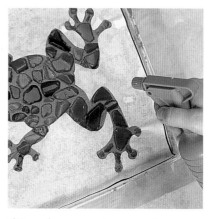

If the surface cracks when you push a piece in, you may spray the surface with water and try again — but only once. If the mix keeps cracking, your hour is probably over and you should stop working.

Using An Embedding Block

Another embedding method involves using a heavy, flat block to embed your tesserae after partially embedding them with your fingers or pencil ereaser. The block levels the tesserae, pushes in hard-to-embed pieces, and usually speeds up the embedding process. My favorite block is a heavy, smooth block of granite, about 6" x 4" x 1" (15cm x 10cm x 25mm), a comfortable size to hold in one hand. You can use a wood block, as in the photographs, or some other heavy, flat weight (but not a brick; it's too heavy). Begin by using it to embed projects that have flat, even pieces. When you're accustomed to using the block, you can use it to embed projects with uneven pieces.

MATERIALS

rubber gloves

prepared mix in mold with
tesserae partially embedded

embedding block

After you've laid out the tesserae on the wet mix and are satisfied with the placement, partially embed them with your fingers. Place the block in the middle of the stone on top of the pieces. Lift it about an inch (25mm) and drop it flat onto the surface. Move the block slightly then lift and drop again. Work your way out from the center, overlapping each time. The pieces will become embedded uniformly and (depending on the material) fairly quickly, so monitor your progress often. Go over the entire surface lightly a few times rather than heavily once or twice, to fully and evenly embed all the mosaic pieces.

I recommend using the embedding block on pebble, stone and glass nuggets because it levels out bumpy, irregular stones. Vibrating or tapping the block while holding it down also helps embed those especially stubborn items. One note of caution: It's easy to over-embed irregularly shaped items, so check your progress often.

The embedding block will probably spread wet mix over your tesserae. If this occurs, sponge off the surface (see Smoothing the Surface on page 35) before you set the stone aside to harden.

tip

Don't use the embedding block on chunky glass tesserae such as in the frog project. The pieces will become covered with wet mix, which will settle into the tiny depressions in the glass. After the mix hardens, it will be nearly impossible to clean off.

Contact Paper Transfer and Embedding Method

There may be times when you lay out a design and get interrupted, or you may want to set a layout aside until another day. You can finish the layout as precisely as possible, use the contact paper as shown below, and instead of trimming off the excess contact paper, replace the paper backing on the contact paper. Your pieces will remain in place.

This technique can also be used to lay out and embed a small design; large projects or designs with lumpy pieces will not work. This is a great technique because it

embeds the pieces exactly the way you positioned them in the first place. It is especially useful for small designs with many tiny, uniformly flat pieces.

Clear contact paper is not paper at all, but vinyl; so don't be confused when I refer to it as "paper" in the instructions. You should test the adhesion of your contact paper before using it for this technique. Less expensive brands of paper may not hold the pieces firmly, causing them to fall off, which will prove to be very frustrating.

MATERIALS

tesserae

Design Template

transparent adhesive-backed vinyl or
contact paper, 10"x 10" (25cm x 25cm)

scissors

rubber gloves

tweezers

mold filled with wet mix

optional: embedding block

1 ➤ Lay out pieces. Lay out your tesserae on the Design Template. Rearrange them until you are satisfied with the design. The way you lay it out now is how it will look on the finished stone.

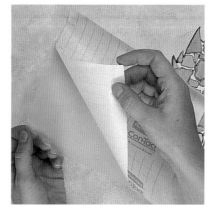

2 ➤ Cut the contact paper to size. Cut a sheet of transparent contact paper large enough to cover the design and leave a 1" (25mm) border all the way around it. Remove the paper backing. Fold over each of the corners to create four places to hold that won't stick to your fingers when you position the paper.

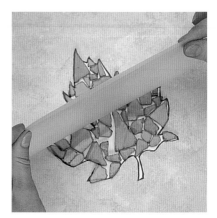

3 ➤ Center the contact paper on the design. With the sticky side out, bend the contact paper in half. Line up the bend with an imaginary horizontal line going through the center of the design. Be careful and confident — you have only one chance. The trick is to lay the contact paper on top of the tesserae without disturbing them. Otherwise, they will shift and stick in the wrong position. Do this and the next two steps in one fluid motion, if possible.

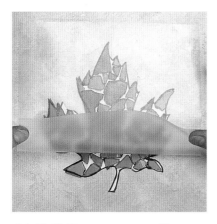

4 ➤ Roll the paper over the pieces. Lower the paper until the bend touches the tesserae. Keep lowering it, rolling the two halves down evenly and lightly onto all the pieces.

5 ➤ Let go. Lower the paper until it is flat on the pieces. Then let go of the paper.

6 ➤ Press each piece. With one finger, touch each of the pieces, making sure that they adhere to the contact paper.

7 ➤ Turn it over. Lift the contact paper and carefully turn it over on the table.

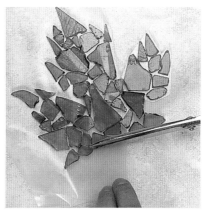

8 ➤ Trim the contact paper. Use scissors to trim the excess paper, staying as close to the outline of the design as possible. If you replace the paper backing, you can more easily move or store your layout. Or you can go ahead and prepare your mold, mix up some concrete and embed the pieces as the next step describes.

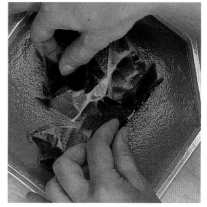

9 ➤ Lay the contact paper on the wet mix. When the wet mix is smooth in the mold, you can transfer the pieces. Place the contact paper on the tabletop with the tesserae on the bottom. Pick it up, bending it in half. Hold it above the prepared mix, then lower it onto the mix surface, rolling the two halves evenly. Position it within the mold edges, resting the pieces and vinyl on the mix surface. If necessary, reposition the sheet now.

Contact Paper Transfer and Embedding Method

➤ continued

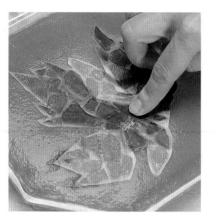

10 ➤ Embed the pieces. Push in the pieces one at time, starting at the center of the design and working your way out.

11 ➤ Use the embedding block. You may instead choose to embed the pieces using the embedding block as described on page 31.

12 ➤ Level the surface. Notice how the wet mix rises between each piece and spreads between all the pieces and the contact paper. This is what you want. The tesserae will look pretty gray and messy, but will clean up easily.

Use your fingertips to smooth out the contact paper so all the pieces look wet and embedded. It's OK if the pieces and the contact paper sink into the mix a bit. Jiggle the mold and turn it, jiggle and turn, and watch the surface level out. Then wait five to ten minutes for the mix to dissolve the contact paper adhesive.

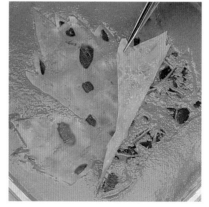

13 ➤ Peel off the contact paper. Use tweezers to slowly peel away the contact paper, which should easily release from the glass. If the paper sticks, lightly spray water on the seam between it and the glass. Soak up extra water with a paper towel.

14 ➤ Embed the stem. Embed any pieces you didn't include in the original layout, such as this stem. Now it's time to clean and smooth the surface.

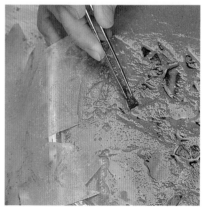

If a small tessera sticks to the contact paper, use the tweezers to replace it.

Smoothing the Surface

When you make a particularly smudged up, messy surface (as the block and contact paper methods are known to do) clean it up before the mix sets—no later than one hour after combining the concrete mix and water.

All your projects should be jiggled, as shown at the bottom of this page. Sponging, however, is optional. Sponge only if you have a particularly messy surface.

sponge or foam paint brush
bowl of water
rubber gloves

Sponging

1 ➤ Wet the sponge. Fill a bowl with water and put on gloves. Wet the sponge and squeeze out most of the water.

2 ➤ Wipe the surface. Lightly wipe the dampened sponge over the entire surface to smooth it and even out the texture. Rinse the sponge often. This adds a very small amount of water to the top layer of the mix which will easily fill any cracks and even out the surface. For your last few strokes, absorb this excess water by rinsing the sponge and squeezing it dry. Spots or pools of water left on the surface may stain or discolor the hardened stone. Now proceed to the next step: jiggling.

Jiggling

3 ➤ Jiggle the mold. Do this step before you make any lines, hand prints or writing in the wet mix. This is your last chance to make a level, smooth surface, if that is what you want.

Make sure the pieces are properly embedded. Now jiggle the mold. It's the same technique you used to smooth out the mix when you prepared it at the outset, but not as vigorously. Hold opposite sides of the mold and jiggle it one to two inches (25-50mm), back and forth, two times in a continuous motion. Notice how the mix unifies and the surface smooths. Rotate the mold and repeat, jiggling as little as possible, just enough to even out the surface.

Too much vibration may cause water to rise to the surface. Use a paper towel to soak up water that may stain or discolor the hardened stone. If jiggling the mold creates a gap around a piece, use a gloved fingertip to smooth over the mix and refill the space. If the jiggling completely submerges a piece, see page 43 for directions on fixing this problem.

If the jiggling seems too risky but the surface needs smoothing, try vibrating the table or tapping the sides of the mold, as shown in the photograph. This may take a little longer, but it will smooth the surface without submerging any precarious pieces.

Incising Lines

Besides decorating your stone with pieces of glass, tile, stone and found objects, you can also embellish it by making impressions: marks, grooves, figures, notches, symbols, lines, prints and furrows, just to name a few. There are countless ways to do this; here are a few of my favorites to get you started.

There is a lot you can do with a plain craft stick or kitchen utensil. You'll get many ideas by experimenting right after you put the mix in the mold before you transfer your tesserae. This is a good time to practice lettering your family name or "Welcome." Write words in different styles and sizes. Use a craft stick with an up-and-down dabbing motion (don't drag the stick), pressing into the surface about ¼" (6mm). If you soak the wooden stick in water, the wet mix won't stick to it. The tool should make a crisp, dry line in the mix. If the line looks wet or keeps filling with water, wait ten or fifteen minutes and try again. A little excess water may be absorbed with a cotton swab.

Other tools to try are cookie cutters, chisel-shaped tools such as a screwdriver or wood chisel (which makes letters that look like calligraphy), pencil tips (for dots) and large rubber stamps with simple, deeply-etched designs. An empty tin can or the lid of a saucepan can be used to stamp a perfect circle. One of my favorite lettering tools is a set of plastic stamps designed for cake decorating. The stamps are pressed into cake frosting as a guide for thin lines of icing. A sign made with these letters is shown on page 16.

MATERIALS

wet mix in a mold
craft stick
miscellaneous kitchen utensils
cookie cutters
pencil
large, thick rubber stamps
cake lettering stamps

The chicken and petroglyph projects have outlines incised around the mosaicked forms. This border highlights the image and adds depth and contrast. Plan for the placement of lines or impressions when you do your initial design. Estimate the amount of space needed and leave it blank until you've embedded all the tesserae. The time to make this line is after the final smoothing and jiggling. Try to make a smooth and flowing line ¼" (6mm) from the tesserae. Do not jiggle the mold again because the lines will disappear!

Impressions by their very nature create fault lines in your hardened stone. The rule is the deeper the incision, the weaker the overall stone. Keep this in mind when considering the stone's function. Wall plaques and decorative garden art are great projects for this technique. A stepping stone with a long line or an outline is at risk for cracking under pressure when someone walks on it. For a strong stepping stone, keep the lines short, such as dashes, dots and letters.

Setting the Stone Aside to Harden

After you've finished embedding, smoothing and possibly incising, move your creation to an out-of-the-way place to harden for two days (48 hours). While the mix is wet, it is important to move the stone by picking up the rigid board underneath the mold. Any bends or creases in the wet mix may create concealed cracks which will set as weakened fault lines. After 48 hours, you can move the stone without the board.

Set the stone in a level place out of direct sunlight and in a moderate temperature for 48 hours. Cover it loosely with plastic, making sure the plastic doesn't touch the wet mix surface or it may leave a permanent stain. Spray the stone with water after 24 hours.

Unmolding a Stone With a Mounting Device

After hardening for 48 hours, your stone may be removed from the mold. This is usually a simple task: turn the mold over and pop the stone out onto a padded surface, such as a folded towel. If you put a wall mounting device on the back of the stone, however, it will stick to the mold and you will have to use greater effort and care.

1 ► **Invert the mold.** Lay the stone face down on an old towel. If your mold is transparent, you will be able to see the tape through the back of the mold.

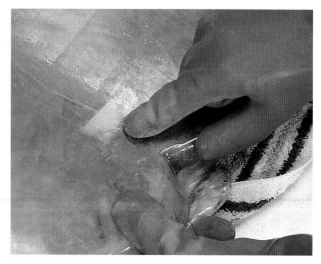

2 ► **Loosen and remove the mold.** Carefully pull the edges of the mold away from the stone all the way around, then start removing the mold. The tape will stick, so the mold must be pried away, Be careful not to damage the stone or crack the mold.

3 ► **Remove the tape.** Remove the tape with the screwdriver tip to reveal the nail hole. Carefully scrape and smooth the opening with the tip of the screwdriver. One or two heavy nails or screws are usually enough to hold a seven- to ten-pound (3.2-4.5kg) stone securely. Depending on the composition of your wall, you may have to add anchors or use masonry screws.

Cleaning and Unmolding the Stone

If you wait much longer than 48 hours to do this, you'll have a difficult if not impossible time cleaning the surface. Set aside 20 to 30 minutes for this series of steps.

MATERIALS

rubber gloves

plastic sheet or newspaper

toothbrush

scouring pad

small bowl of water

safety glasses

paper clip, nail, or other pointed tool

old towel

dust mask

screwdriver

5-gallon (3.8l) bucket

garden hose and water source

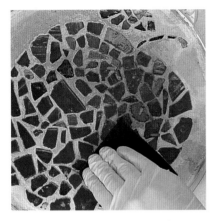 

1 ➤ Gently scrub the surface. About 48 hours after you set you stone aside to harden, you will need to clean the mix from the tesserae. Now you may lift the mold without the board. Inspect the mosaic surface to see if any of the pieces have a film or layer of concrete over them. If so, put on gloves and dip a toothbrush or scouring pad in water. Gently scrub the entire surface, both the concrete and the tesserae, until the excess concrete lifts off. Use as much water as you need. The concrete is still "green," which means that it is hard but it can still crumble, so go slowly and gently. Most glass and tile surfaces are pretty tough and can handle scouring for a short time. Use your judgment about scouring painted china and other delicate surfaces.

2 ➤ Define edges with paper clip. Use safety glasses because this process may cause chips of concrete to fly up. Scrape dried mix from the edges of the tesserae with the sharp tip of a straightened paper clip or other pointed tool. Clearly defined edges make a world of difference in the finished look of your mosaic design. Clean up incised lines, if necessary.

Drain excess water into a large bucket, not down the drain.

3 ➤ Remove the mold. Lay the stone face down on an old towel. Carefully separate the stone from the edges of the mold. Remove the mold from the stone.

4 ➤ Scrape the edges. Keep your safety glasses on and put on a dust mask. Hold an old screwdriver at a 45° angle to scrape and smooth the crusty lip of the stone all the way around. This edge can be very sharp when it comes out of the mold, so be careful.

5 ➤ Rinse the stone and set it aside to cure. Remove your glasses and mask. The easiest way to rinse off the stone is to spray it outdoors with a garden hose. You can also pour clean water over the stone, holding it over a large bucket or pan. Don't pour the water from the bucket down any drain; pour it outdoors and rinse the bucket clean.

Your project is now complete! Set it aside to finish hardening.

Elevating and Curing the Stone

If concrete dries too fast, it shrinks, causing it to lose its strength and compromising its durability. Cracks may form in the concrete and tesserae may pop out. This is why we slow down the drying and hardening process, commonly called curing, by covering the concrete loosely with plastic and watering it frequently. (If plastic touches the concrete, it can cause permanent stains.) For the stone to cure evenly, air must circulate freely around it, so the stone should be elevated on a rack or resting on several pencils.

After you have cleaned, unmolded and rinsed off your stone, set it on a nonporous rack or on several pencils, out of sunlight and loosely covered with plastic. Spray it with water every 24 hours for five more days, then use a soft cloth to polish individual mosaic pieces. Wait seven more days before applying pressure. The stone continues to cure for another 28 days.

tip

Shells, stones, frosted glass and marble may be enhanced with a coating of oil or wax after your project has cured.

Caring For Your Stone

Several conditions influence the strength and durability of concrete: humidity and temperature during mixing, the amount of water used in the mix, and the curing conditions. Concrete mixed with as little water as possible in ideal circumstances (moderate temperature, no direct sun or high wind) and kept moist while curing should last for a very long time. To reduce the chances of cracks, a stepping stone path should be embedded flush with the ground and placed on a firm and even 2" (5cm) bed of crushed gravel or sand.

The concrete surface will change with time. You may leave it to age naturally or you may clean it occasionally. White powdery stains may appear on the surface of the hardened concrete that are difficult or impossible to remove, but you may try to scrub them off with a stiff brush and household detergent and water or trisodium phosphate. De-icer or rock salt will cause the concrete to deteriorate, so keep these off your stone.

Many people want to protect their stone from the weather and stains by waterproofing it. Sealing a mosaic concrete stone is a topic of controversy, and I cannot make any guarantees about fully protecting your stone. Even if you seal it fully and properly, damage may still occur; water may seep in, stains may set. When water freezes it expands, so wet cured concrete can crack in freezing weather. Many types of concrete sealant are available at hardware stores. The sealant is for the concrete only—the stone

bottom, sides and the joints between the tesserae on the top. If you cover the tesserae with sealant, you run the risk of changing their appearance. Wait 28 days before sealing your stone, after it has fully cured.

I recommend that you bring your mosaic creations indoors during extreme weather, or place them in a protected spot such as on a covered porch or on a sunroom wall. I live in the Pacific Northwest where it rarely freezes, and if a summer day reaches 85°, it's considered a heat wave. I can leave my stones out all year long unsealed. In other parts of the world, "Mother Nature" can be even tougher than concrete!

Tesserae may crack, loosen or pop out of the concrete bed for several reasons. They may not have been fully embedded in the first place; they may have been too thin to get a grip; plastic or rubber pieces didn't bond with the concrete; or the concrete cured too quickly. You may glue pieces back in place, but you must find the right kind of glue for the specific material you're replacing. For example, gluing glass to concrete requires one kind of glue, but gluing metal to concrete may require another. Weld-bond is a strong and reliable glue for many things. Read the glue label to be certain it can handle the job.

Finally, although concrete is almost indestructible, these cast projects will break if dropped. Treat them with care, as you would any work of art, and you will enjoy them for a very long time.

Quick Fixes

Occasionally, you may have an unexpected problem while making your mosaic stone. If you learn about the most common problems and how to handle them before these events occur, you'll be better able to expect the unexpected! All of these problems have happened to me at one time or another, so I have learned to make the best of these situations.

As I said before, concrete is a very forgiving medium while it is still wet and plastic. You can prove this to yourself after you have poured and smoothed the mix for a project. Poke a couple of holes or make a gash with the putty knife, then see how easy it is to smooth it, jiggle it and start all over again.

Because it's common for beginners to create a mix using too much water, before you make your first stone, set aside a small amount of dry mix in a covered plastic container that you can sprinkle in your mix if you accidentally add too much water. You can also mix some of this with a little water to patch holes and depressions that may occur in a hardened stone, although it may not exactly match the new stone's color.

You will find it helpful to set aside a spoonful of wet mix at the start of projects that include tile, broken cups, rocks and pieces with uneven edges or irregular shapes. When embedded, these items usually leave large craters in the mix. After you finish embedding, you can use this extra mix to fill holes and patch gaps rather than stealing mix from another part of the stone, which is a good technique for patching smaller craters.

Excess Water

Occasionally you may find excess water rising to the surface of the mix. Sometimes this happens because the stone has been jiggled too much. Other times, it happens because too much water was added in the first place, as is the case here. I like to get rid of excess water so that I can clearly see the outline of each piece, and to avoid having permanent stains left on the stone after it has hardened. For small spots, use a cotton swab. For larger wet areas, lightly lay a piece of paper towel on top of the wet area. Peel off the paper towel and continue with your project.

Cracks in the Wet Mix

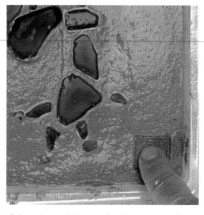

If the mix cracks in a radiating pattern when you make an impression or push in a mosaic piece, it means the concrete is drying out.

If one hour is not yet up, spray the surface lightly once or twice with water. If necessary, smooth or erase the impression with a wet, gloved finger and start again. Work quickly.

If one hour is up, it's too late. The concrete is hardening and you risk permanently setting cracks in the stone. Stop what you're doing. Spray the surface lightly with water, smooth and erase the impression with a wet, gloved finger, and set the stone aside to cure.

Sharp or Exposed Glass Edges

If there are sharp edges protruding above the surface of the hardened stone, you can sand them down with fine-grit sandpaper or a sanding block after the stone has cured.

Mosaic Piece Embedded too Deeply

You've just finished embedding all the pieces, cleaned up the surface and given your mold a final jiggle. As you're adjusting the position of one last piece, it suddenly sinks into the wet mix. Now what?

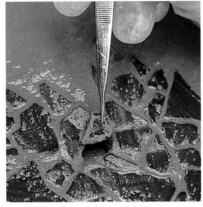

1 ➤ Remove the piece. Use tweezers to carefully retrieve the sunken piece. Try not to disturb the surrounding area. Wipe off the piece and set it aside.

2 ➤ Take some mix. Now you're going to take some mix from the edge of the stone where it won't be missed. It is very important that the mix still be in a wet, plastic state so that it will easily blend in. Use the opposite end of the tweezers to skim off a small amount of mix near the edge of the mold.

3 ➤ Patch the hole. Patch the hole with the extra mix until it is slightly over-filled. Scoop mix from a different edge if you need more. Tamp and smooth the patch with a gloved finger. Lightly skim the surface with the putty knife to smooth out the areas. Jiggle the mold a few times, being careful not to let other pieces sink in.

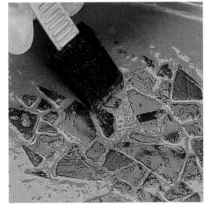

4 ➤ Smooth the patch. Use a damp sponge to lightly smooth the patched area until it is level with the rest of the surface.

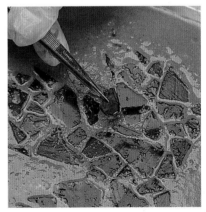

5 ➤ Replace the piece. Use the tweezers to replace the piece and embed it. Smooth the area with a sponge and jiggle if needed.

Fruit Path

> Adorn your garden or yard with a colorful pathway of mosaic fruit stepping stones. These five designs are bold and easy to make. If this is your first time making a mosaic stone, I recommend glass tesserae, stained glass fragments or vitreous glass tiles.

You will be introduced to several basic techniques with the apple design; the pear and bananas are made in a similar way. The designs for the grapes and raspberries add another mosaic element, glass nuggets; and a new tool, the embedding block, for leveling a bumpy surface.

For variations, consider changing the colors: a pale green apple, purple grapes and a red or yellow pear. Another idea is to add wall mounting devices (see page 21) and hang the plaques as a group in the kitchen or back hallway. You can even "think small" and use these designs to make paperweights for your desk or coasters for the patio. If you "think large," you could make a fruit tabletop.

MATERIALS

round stepping stone mold
12" x 12" x 1½"
(30cm x 30cm x 38mm)

pencil with eraser

craft knife

scissors

stained glass: opaque red and translucent dark green for the apple; opaque light green and translucent dark green for the pear; opaque yellow and translucent dark brown for bananas; transparent dark green for grapes; translucent dark green for raspberries

medium-size round glass nuggets: 45 transparent light green for grapes; 42 transparent red for raspberries

rigid board for each stone

dust mask

rubber gloves

7 lbs. (3.2kg) stepping stone concrete mix for each stone

mixing bowl

mixing tool

2 cups (472ml) water for each stone

3" (75mm) putty knife

sponge and small bowl of water

embedding block for grapes and raspberries

Apple

1 ➤ **Enlarge the pattern.** Use a copy machine to enlarge the apple pattern from page 51 to fit your mold. For a 12" (30cm) mold, enlarge the pattern 200%, then enlarge the copy 200%. Make a second copy of the enlarged pattern.

2 ➤ **Make templates.** Use a craft knife to cut out the apple shape from one pattern and trim the outside edge to fit your mold; this is your Mold Template. The cut-out shape is your Design Template, or you can use the extra pattern. See page 17 for more information on templates.

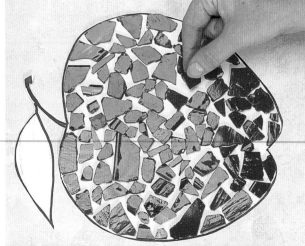

3 ➤ Outline the apple. Arrange red glass tesserae on the Design Template, starting with the outline and staying within the line. See pages 18-20 for more information on laying out your design.

4 ➤ Fill in the apple. Finish arranging the red pieces, filling in the entire apple.

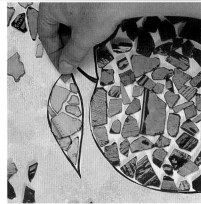

5 ➤ Add leaf tips. Start by finding the key pieces for the leaf: one pointed piece to fit in each of the two corners.

6 ➤ Finish the leaf. Outline the leaf and fill it in. Set aside three or four small pieces of green glass for the stem, but do not put them in place yet.

7 ➤ Prepare the mold and mix. Place the mold on a board. Put on a dust mask and gloves and prepare the mix as described on pages 23-26. Check the time or set a timer for one hour. You have 45 minutes to one hour to complete the process.

8 ➤ Place the Mold Template on the wet mix surface. Be sure it is centered.

9 ➤ Transfer the outline and key pieces. Transfer the pieces to the mix surface in the same order that you laid out the design, starting with the outline and key pieces. Be careful to keep pieces inside the paper edge. Refer to page 28 for a full description of this process.

10 ➤ Fill in. Now fill in the apple and the leaf, arranging and rearranging pieces until they are evenly spaced. Don't push the pieces into the mix yet; just leave them lying on the surface.

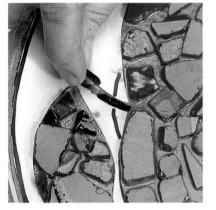

11 ➤ Make the apple stem. Get the green glass you set aside earlier and embed it on edge. See the Tip on page 48 for details.

12 ➤ Remove the template. Slowly peel off the paper template. Stand back and squint to see if any changes are needed: Is the outline smooth and readable as an apple? Are there any holes in the mosaic layout that need filling? If you need to make other changes, make them now.

13 ➤ Embed the tesserae. Begin embedding the pieces, as described on pages 29-31. Begin at the center of the apple and work your way out. Push straight down. You'll need to go over all the pieces several times until every piece is fully embedded: not too deep (submerged), not too high (resting on the surface), but just right (flush with the mix). The surface will be uneven.

14 ➤ Make final changes and jiggle. Stand back, look at the stone and squint. Fill in any gray spaces or gaps with glass pieces. Make sure all pieces are evenly embedded. Gently jiggle the mold as described on page 35.

15 ➤ Set the stone aside to harden for 48 hours. Cover the stone loosely with plastic. Use the board to pick up the stone and move it to a safe location. Spray it with water after 24 hours.

16 ➤ Clean up the stone. When 48 hours are up, gently scrub excess concrete from the tesserae as described on page 39. Remove the stone from the mold and round off the edges. Rinse the stone well.

17 ➤ Elevate the stone and let it cure. Let the stone cure, elevated on a rack or on pencils for five more days. Cover it loosely with plastic to cure slowly, which make a sturdier stone. Spray it with water every 24 hours. After five days, the stone may be used, as long as no pressure is applied to it for an additional seven days.

Pear

The directions for the pear are similar to those for the apple, but the pear has both concave and convex curves. Arrange light green tesserae on the Design Template to outline the pear, then fill it in, staying inside the line. Try to follow the curves with similarly curved tesserae.

Place key pieces for the leaves: find six dark green pointed pieces to fit into the leaf tips, then fill in the centers. Select eight to ten small dark green pieces to use later for the stem, but don't place them yet.

Position the Mold Template, then transfer the mosaic pieces to the wet mix surface in the same order.

When you make the stem, start next to the pear and leaves and work your way out.

Before you embed a piece, you may want to reposition it slightly. I have a large pair of tweezers that come in handy for this, but you could also use either end of a pencil.

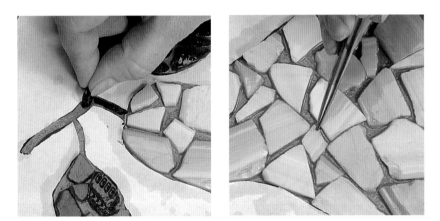

tip

When you need a thin, uniform line, embed glass pieces "on edge." Look for pieces of broken glass that are long and narrow, or triangular, rather than round or square. Choose a piece that has one long edge that is especially straight, which is the edge you want showing on the top side. Pick a piece that is about ½" (1cm) wide that will not go all the way through to the bottom of the mold. Start embedding the first stem piece on edge next to the fruit. Embed the second piece so it touches the first, and so on, working your way away from the fruit until the stem is the correct length. Embed the top edges flush with the mix surface.

Bananas

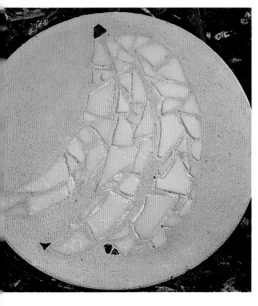

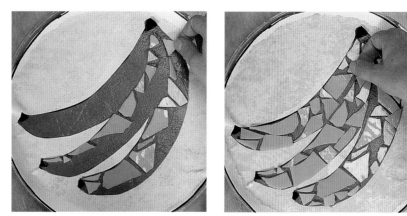

The long, curved shape of the bananas requires a slightly different layout technique from that of the apple and pear. Start with the left outline of each fruit, then the right outline, then fill in the center. Try to use slightly curved glass edges to follow the outlines of each banana. Find four small pieces of dark brown glass with squared-off ends; then place one at the top and one at the end of each banana.

Grapes

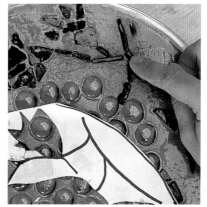

When you cut out the Mold Template for the grapes, the stems may be too narrow to cut; so you may choose to leave them uncut and embed those pieces after the template has been removed.

Arrange 45 light green glass nuggets on the Design Template, placing them so that they touch. If the nuggets are oval, line them up vertically. Next, position the leaf points, then the leaf outlines. Fill in the leaf centers.

To emb the glass, use your fingertips, the embedding block, or a combination of the two. If you want a bumpy surface, emb the glass nuggets at least two-thirds of the way. For a more level surface, use the embedding block over the entire surface. See page 31 for more details on using an embedding block.

If you did not cut out the stems on the Design Template, lay it back on the mix below the stems. Use a craft stick or pencil point to draw the stems. Make a line or series of dots using an up-and-down dabbing motion. First indicate the main stem, then an off-shoot line to the grapes and finally a line to each leaf. Use the line for placing and embedding the green glass on edge.

Raspberries

When you arrange red glass nuggets on the Design Template for each berry, arrange fourteen nuggets touching each other in four parallel rows: 3-4-4-3, then push them together until the shape rounds out and fits inside the outline. Place the large leaf points, outline the leaves, then fill them in. Select nine to twelve triangular, similarly-sized pieces of green glass to be used as small leaves. Choose eight to ten small green pieces for the stems and set them aside.

Transfer the pieces as you did for the grapes. Make sure the glass nuggets are touching. To save time, I didn't cut the small leaves and stems out of the Design Template.

If you want a slightly bumpy surface, embed the glass nuggets at least two-thirds of the way using just your fingertips. Then push in the green glass pieces. For a more level surface, use the embedding block for the entire surface. See page 31 for more details on using the block. For embedding very small pieces, a pencil eraser head is very helpful.

The stems for the raspberries are done the same way as the stems for the grapes. Using a craft stick or pencil point with an up-and-down dabbing motion, make a light line or series of dots connecting the middle berry and the clump of leaves, then the two offshoot lines to the other berries. Use the lines as guides for placing and embedding the green glass on edge for the stems.

To enlarge these patterns for a 12" (30 cm) mold, use a copy machine to enlarge them 200%. Then enlarge the copies 200%.

River Rock Garden Path

Often, the simpler the design, the more elegant and versatile it is — plus it is easier and faster to make! The geometric designs of this project may be combined in many ways to create various patterns as shown on page 56. To find out what is most pleasing to you, make copies of the small patterns, cut them out and arrange them on a table until you find a pattern that pleases you and fits the number of stones you need for your path. A path may be two or more stones wide, and your molds may be square, hexagonal or round. Rocks in all shapes, sizes and colors may be found at garden stores or your local creek. In this project you will see how easy it is to change the color of your concrete to coordinate with the color of your stones.

MATERIALS

square stepping stone mold
12" x 12" x 1½"
(30cm x 30cm x 38mm)

pencil with eraser

craft knife or scissors

Indonesian river rocks, about 1 lb.
(454g), average size 1" (25mm) long

rigid board

dust mask

rubber gloves

7 lbs. (3.2kg) stepping stone
concrete mix

2 oz. (28g) packet of
sandstone-colored dry pigment

mixing bowl

mixing tool

2 cups (472ml) water

3" (75mm) putty knife

embedding block

1 ▶ Enlarge the pattern. Use a copy machine to enlarge the pattern to fit your mold. Make two copies of the enlarged pattern.

2 ▶ Make the templates. Follow the directions on page 17 for cutting out your templates. For this project, cut on the outside of the line or a bit farther out to accommodate the rocks. (Too big an opening is better than too small. You'll see why when you remove the template after the rocks are in place.) This pattern with the cut-out area is your Mold Template. The extra enlarged pattern is your Design Template.

3 ▶ Lay out rocks on the Design Template. Try to select rocks of similar width. With this pattern, I suggest starting in the middle and working your way out, positioning longer rocks with the direction of the spiral line. Space them end-to-end and touching, so that the spiral (or other design) will "read" as one continuous line.

Another method of laying out irregularly-shaped tesserae is to lay the Mold Template in a shallow box of sand. Push the pieces into the sand to lay out the design, as in the Lizard project on page 96.

4 ➤ Prepare the mold and the mix. If you wish to add colorant to your stone, see page 27 for instructions. Place the mold on a board. Put on your dust mask and gloves and prepare the mix as described on pages 23-26. Set aside a heaping spoonful of wet mix in a small plastic container before emptying the rest into the mold. You may need this extra mix for patching depressions. Check the time or set a timer for one hour. Your mix will start setting up 45 to 60 minutes after it has been mixed with water. This should be plenty of time for you to complete the simple rock design.

5 ➤ Place the Mold Template on the mix. Position the Mold Template on the wet mix surface and smooth it down. Always check the template at this point to be sure it is positioned the way you want it. The mosaic design edges should be a minimum of ¼" (6mm) from the edges of the mold.

6 ➤ Transfer the rocks. Transfer the river rocks, beginning at the center of the design and working your way out. The rocks should be touching because after they are embedded the curved surface will cause them to appear as if they were spaced farther apart. This happens any time you use rounded mosaic pieces.

7 ➤ Remove the template. Slowly peel off the paper template. If rocks overlap the paper, carefully lift the paper around them. Stand back to see if any adjustments are needed. If so, do that now.

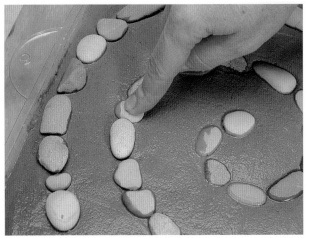

8 ➤ Begin embedding the rocks. Start in the center of the design and begin pushing in the rocks with your fingertips. Push straight down. A little seesaw action will help embed the longer pieces. Embed the rocks at least two-thirds of the way.

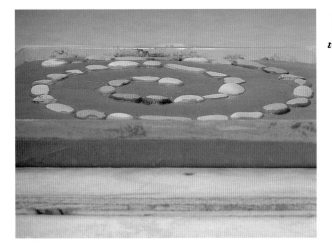

You may stop embedding now if you like this bumpy surface. Skip to step 10 to complete your stone. Here the partially embedded rocks make the stone rougher to walk on, but they show off the varied rock shapes and create a continuous line.

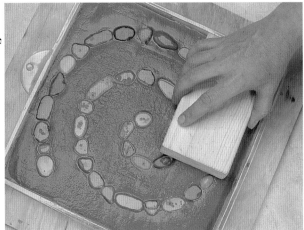

9 ➤ Level the surface. You can choose to make a more level surface by using the embedding block as described on page 31. This step will evenly embed your rounded rocks. The only drawback to this choice is that your rocks will be more deeply submerged in the wet mix, making the spaces between them larger and the result may be that your design loses some of its feeling of continuity.

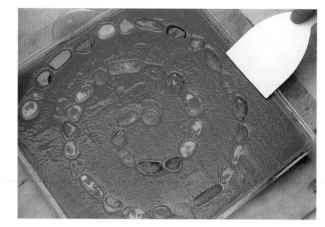

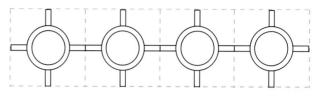

10 ➤ Fill gaps and valleys. When you've finished embedding, look closely at the stone. You may see a few small valleys or gaps alongside some rocks that you may want to fill in or smooth over with wet concrete. You have several choices:

✳ Use a sponge to fill in and smooth the surface as described on page 35.

✳ Patch the areas using the mix you set aside. See page 43.

✳ Take a bit of wet mix from the edge of the stone if you have just a small area to fill.

✳ Just leave it alone. (This option is my favorite.) The hills and valleys make a more textured and varied surface.

After you've smoothed the surface, gently jiggle the mold as described on page 35.

11 ➤ Set the stone aside to harden for 48 hours. See page 37 for details. Cover the stone loosely with plastic, and use the board to transfer it to a safe location. Spray it with water after 24 hours.

12 ➤ Clean up the stone. After 48 hours, gently scrub excess concrete from the rocks as described on page 39. Remove the stone from the mold and round off the edges. Rinse the stone well.

13 ➤ Elevate the stone and let it cure. Let the stone cure elevated on a rack or on pencils, for five more days. Cover it loosely with plastic so that it cures slowly, making a sturdier stone. Spray it with water every 24 hours. After five days the stone will be ready for use, as long as no pressure is applied to it for an additional seven days.

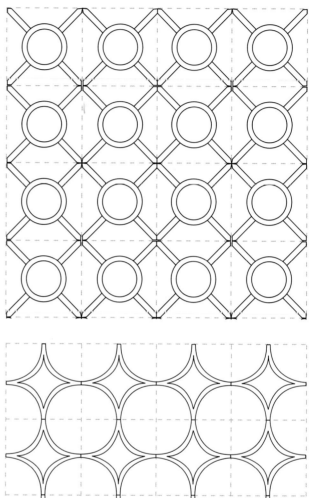

The designs on the following page can be combined in many ways to create patterns when the stones are set in a line to make a path or set next to each other to create a paved area in your yard.

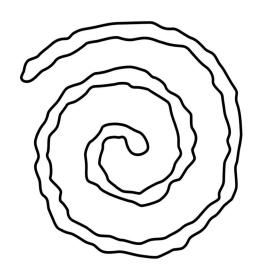

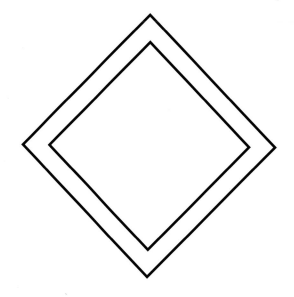

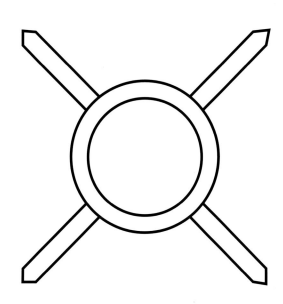

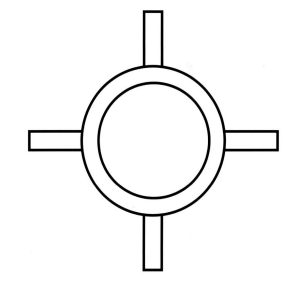

To enlarge these patterns for a
12" (30cm) mold, use a copy
machine to enlarge them 200%.
Then take the enlarged copies
and enlarge them 200%.

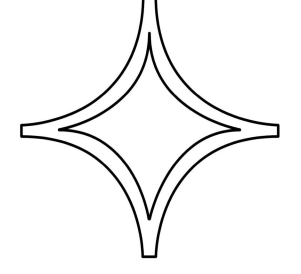

Reflective Heart Wall Stone

A broken mirror isn't bad luck for a mosaicist! Mirror pieces can be used to add sparkle to any mosaic design as an accent or used overall as in this heart-shaped wall plaque. Because this is a decorative stone, I was able to use several oversized mosaic pieces larger than the 2" x 2" (5cm x 5cm) maximum glass size for stepping stones.

Designs which cover the entire surface of the stone are quick and fun to make. There are two ways to proceed: make only one template by tracing the mold onto a piece of paper, or be spontaneous and daring and use no template at all! Simply empty the wet mix into the mold and start arranging and embedding.

I used black dry pigment to darken the concrete. You may want to try a different color, such as red or blue, to coordinate with the colors in the room where your plaque will hang. You could also make a set of small coaster-size stones decorated with mosaic mirror bits to scatter in your garden beds (see the last project in the book for using deli containers as small molds). Mirror tiles could be used to outline a stepping stone. And of course, this heart mold can be used with other mosaic materials, such as broken china or tumbled glass.

MATERIALS

heart-shaped stepping stone mold
12" x 12" x 1½"
(30cm x 30cm x 38mm)

paper

pencil with eraser

broken mirror pieces

acrylic spray

rigid board

mounting device:
2"x 2" (5cm x 5cm) cardboard square
3"x 2" (8cm x 5cm) piece of duct tape

dust mask

rubber gloves

7 lbs. (3.2kg)
stepping stone concrete mix

optional: 2 oz. (58g) package
black dry pigment

mixing bowl

mixing tool

2 cups (472ml) water

3" (75mm) putty knife

1 ► **Seal the mirror pieces.** Spray the backs of the pieces of mirror with two light coats of acrylic spray. This prevents the silvering from being damaged by the wet concrete. If your mirror is not yet broken in pieces, follow the instructions on pages 12-13.

2 ► **Make one template.** If you want to use a template, trace the mold you're using onto a piece of paper to create the Design Template. You will not need a Mold Template for this project.

3 ► **Lay out the mirror pieces on the template.** Arrange the broken mirror pieces on the template, wearing gloves to protect against cuts. Begin with the key pieces at the point and V-shape, then start outlining the outer edge. Follow the gradual curve of the border with slightly curved pieces. Then fill in the center.

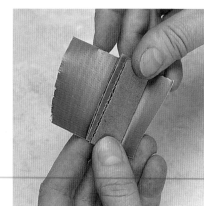
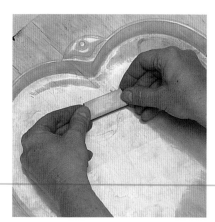

4 ➤ Prepare the mold and the mix. If you're making a wall plaque, follow the directions on page 21 for making a mounting device. Place the mold on a board and prepare the mix as described on pages 23-26. I added black dry pigment to the mix as described on page 27 for more contrast with the mirror pieces.

Check the time or set a timer for one hour.

7 ➤ Embed the pieces. When the pieces are where you want them, begin embedding them. Push straight down.

In cases when your fingers are too big for especially tiny pieces, use the eraser end of a pencil to push the piece straight down into the mix. The rubber keeps the pencil from slipping.

5 ➤ Position key pieces. Transfer mirror pieces to the wet mix surface, starting with the point and V-shape.

6 ➤ Place outline pieces. Next, outline the heart shape placing pieces an even distance from the edge all the way around. Let the pieces just rest on the mix surface for now. Fill in the rest of the shape, arranging and rearranging as you please. I like to use a variety of sizes and shapes for a more interesting design.

8 ➤ Fill in spaces. When you've finished embedding all the pieces, stand back and look at the spacing — is it fairly consistent? Add pieces to any gray spaces or gaps that need them.

9 ➤ Jiggle the mold. Gently jiggle the mold, leveling and smoothing the surface and pieces.

10 ➤ Set the stone aside to harden. Cover the stone loosely with plastic and set it aside for 48 hours. Spray it with water after 24 hours. Be sure the plastic is loose; if it touches the cement it may leave a stain.

11 ➤ Clean up the stone. After 48 hours, gently scrub excess concrete from the mirror pieces. As you remove the stone from the mold, the duct tape will stick to the bottom of the mold and will have to be loosened as the stone releases, as described on page 38. Round off the edges as described on page 39. Rinse the stone well.

12 ➤ Elevate the stone and let it cure. Let the stone cure, elevated on a rack or on pencils, for five more days. Cover it loosely with plastic so that it cures slowly, which makes a sturdier stone. Spray it with water every 24 hours. After five days, the stone will be ready for hanging.

tip

Use a tray to hold and sort your tesserae. It will be easier to put them away and to keep colors separate.

Maple Leaf

This is one of my favorite designs. I have made several of these 8" (20cm) stones, each one in a different color of glass. I have them outside propped up on my kitchen steps. If you choose to make these stones the size shown here, you will need to use smaller tesserae. Small triangular key pieces help create the distinctive maple leaf shape. Because of its small size, this project lends itself well to the contact paper transfer method (see page 32). You could make this design with multicolored instead of solid-colored maple leaves. Another idea is to photocopy and enlarge leaves from other types of trees and make a stepping stone path with one of each type of leaf.

MATERIALS

octagonal stepping stone mold
8" x 8" x 2" (20cm x 20cm x 5cm)

pencil with eraser

scissors

craft knife

tumbled frosted red-orange
stained glass

rigid board

dust mask

rubber gloves

3½ lbs. (1.6kg)
stepping stone concrete mix

mixing bowl

mixing tool

1 cup (236ml) water

3" (75mm) putty knife

1 ➤ Enlarge the pattern. Use a copy machine to enlarge the maple leaf pattern to fit your mold. Make two copies or just use the cut-out leaf from the Mold Template as your Design Template.

2 ➤ Make the templates. Place your mold on the paper template, centering it over the design. Trace the mold with a pencil. Use scissors to cut out along the traced line. With a craft knife, cut out the leaf design. This is your Mold Template.

3 ➤ Lay out key pieces on the design template. Maple leaves have many toothy points on the edges. Look for triangular glass pieces to be the key pieces, which you should place first.

4 ➤ Outline the leaf and fill it in. Arrange the tesserae on the Design Template, starting with the three large leaf points. Add the other points; then outline the shape, staying within the line. Finish arranging pieces by filling in the leaf.

5 ➤ Prepare the mold and the mix. Place your mold on a board. Put on a dust mask and gloves and prepare the mix as described on pages 23-26. Check the time or set a timer for one hour.

6 ➤ Place the mold template on the wet mix surface. Be sure the design is centered. Smooth down the template.

7 ➤ Transfer key pieces. Start transferring your tesserae, starting with the three main leaf points.

8 ➤ Transfer the outline pieces and fill in. Outline the rest of the leaf. Be careful to keep pieces inside the edge of the paper cutout. Finish filling in the rest of the design.

tip

The small scale of this pattern lends itself well to the contact paper transferring and embedding method. Follow the directions on pages 32-34 if you want to use this method.

9 ➤ Make the stem. Select three to four small, narrow pieces of glass each with one long, straight edge. With the straight edge up, embed the first piece adjacent to the leaf, creating a glass line as the leaf stem. Continue the line with a second piece of glass on edge touching the first piece, and so on until the stem is complete.

10 ➤ Remove the template. Carefully peel away the template. Step back and look at the outline of the design and the spacing of the pieces. You may see a few gray spaces that still need a piece of glass. Add those pieces now.

11 ➤ Embed the glass. When you have all the pieces where you want them, begin embedding. Push straight down. See pages 29-34 for more information on embedding.

12 ➤ Jiggle the mold. Gently jiggle the mold to level the surface. Follow the directions on page 35.

13 ➤ Set the stone aside to harden for 48 hours. Pick up the board to move the stone to a safe location. Cover the stone loosely with plastic and spray it with water after 24 hours.

14 ➤ Clean up the stone. After 48 hours, gently scrub excess concrete from the tesserae as described on page 39. Remove the stone from the mold and round off the edges. Rinse the stone well.

15 ➤ Elevate the stone and let it cure. Let the stone cure, elevated on a rack or on pencils, for five more days. Cover it loosely with plastic so that it cures slowly, which makes a sturdier stone. Spray it with water every 24 hours. After five days the stone will be ready for use, as long as no pressure is applied to it for an additional seven days.

To enlarge this pattern for an 8" (20cm) octagonal mold, use a copy machine to enlarge it 200%.

Chicken

> Chickens and roosters are popular motifs, especially for kitchen decor. I decided to get the chicken out of the kitchen and into the garden by putting her on a stepping stone. Even though this is a very detailed project, it's not complicated if you break the design into several smaller shapes. You won't need much yellow or red glass for this design, but have extra on hand so you have plenty to break, sort through, then break again, to create a variety of tiny pointed pieces to use.

I thought of a few variations, and I'm sure that you can think of others. Instead of white glass, use white tile or gravel. Make another stone reversing the image so you have a pair of chickens facing each other. If you make the chicken smaller, you can add your house number using contrasting glass pieces and hang it on your house or place it near the curb.

MATERIALS

round stepping stone mold
12" x 1½" (30cm x 38mm)

pencil with eraser

scissors

craft knife

opaque white, translucent red and translucent yellow stained glass

1 pea-size black glass bead

rigid board

dust mask

rubber gloves

7 lbs. (3.2kg)
stepping stone concrete mix

mixing bowl

mixing tool

2 cups (472ml) water

3" (75mm) putty knife

craft stick

tweezers

1 ➤ Enlarge the pattern. Use a copy machine to enlarge the chicken pattern on page 71. For a 12" (30cm) mold, enlarge it 200%.

2 ➤ Make the templates. Place your mold on the enlarged pattern, centering it over the design. Trace the mold with pencil and cut along the line with scissors. Use a craft knife to cut out the chicken. This is your Mold Template. Use an extra copy of the pattern for your Design Template, or use the cut-out chicken shape.

3 ➤ Lay out the tesserae on the template. With practice, you'll discover the order you prefer for laying out your pieces. For beginners, I suggest the following sequence:

＊ Set aside eight to ten small white pieces for the chicken head.

＊ Select and place the key pieces on the Design Template, beginning with the red pieces on the head and the yellow beak and legs.

＊ Place four to five oval or rectangular white wing pieces of similar size across the center of the figure.

＊ Put several small pointed white pieces up and down the chicken's ruffled tail end.

＊ Follow the outline of the figure from its neck down.

＊ Now arrange the small white head pieces you set aside earlier. Be sure to surround the space for the eye with white, however small the pieces. Don't put the eye in now, because it will roll off the table.

＊ Finally, fill in the rest of the figure, leaving a space of ⅜" (9mm) below the wings for an incised wing line.

4 ➤ Prepare the mold and mix. Place the mold on a board. Put on a dust mask and gloves and prepare the mix as described on pages 23-26. Check the time or set a timer for one hour.

5 ➤ Practice making lines. If this is your first time incising lines in the mix, practice making a few lines now. Use a craft stick or a metal tool. When you've practiced for a few minutes, smooth and jiggle the mold to erase the practice lines.

6 ➤ Place the mold template on the wet mix surface. Position the Mold Template on the wet mix surface and smooth it down.

7 ➤ Lay out the tesserae on the mix. Transfer the tesserae in the same order as in Step 3, beginning with the combs, beak and feet. Now you can put in that eye.

8 ➤ Transfer the wings. Next, position the wing pieces in the middle of the chicken's body.

9 ➤ Transfer the outlines. Lay in the ruffled tail and the outline from the neck down.

10 ➤ Fill in the head. Take a few minutes to arrange the tiny white pieces for the head. Tweezers are helpful for this small scale work. Then fill in everywhere but below the wing.

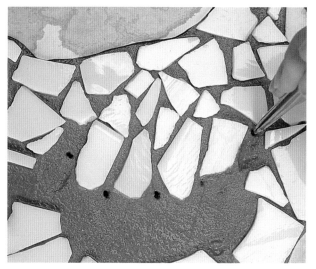

11 ➤ Rough in the wing line. Using the tweezers or a pencil point, make a few small dots below the wings pieces to mark the ends of the scallops of the wing line.

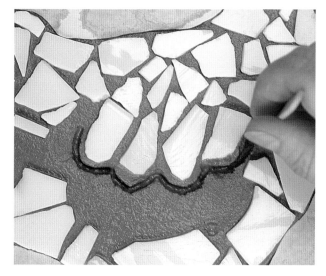

12 ➤ Draw the wing line. Use a craft stick to make a shallow line. Instead of dragging the tool through the wet mix, connect the dots using an up-and-down dabbing motion. Keep ⅛" to ¼" (3mm to 6mm) away from the glass. It doesn't have to be perfect now; you'll go over it again at the very end.

13 ➤ Fill in. Finish filling in the chicken figure with white glass. Is the spacing fairly consistent? If any rearranging or fine-tuning is needed, do it now.

14 ➤ Remove the template. Carefully peel away the template. Some glass pieces may overlap the paper; if so, carefully lift the paper around them. Stand back and take a look. Is the tail outline ruffled? Is the rest of the outline smooth? Finalize the placement of pieces.

15 ➤ Embed the pieces. Begin embedding pieces, pushing straight down. It's OK if the wing line becomes blurred; you'll come back to it later. The pencil eraser head is helpful for pushing in tiny pieces. Embed all the glass.

16 ➤ Smooth and jiggle the mold. Gently jiggle and tap the mold now, smoothing and leveling the glass pieces and the surface. This is the last chance to smooth because after you make lines in the mix, the mold can't be vibrated without erasing the lines.

17 ➤ Incise the outline and wing line. With your craft stick, incise a line all the way around the chicken. Use a dabbing, up-and-down motion, pushing the tool about ¼" (6mm) into the mix. Make the impression a consistent distance from the figure's outline, ⅛" to ¼" (3mm to 6mm) away from the glass. Keep the line simple and smooth. It should look crisp and dry. If it doesn't, wait ten minutes and try again.

18 ➤ Add tail feathers. To soften the tail line, make eight to ten ¼" (6mm) lines at different angles extending from the figure.

19 ➤ Redraw the wing line. If it's been less than an hour since you added water to your dry mix, go over the wing line you made earlier. You may need go over all the lines two or three times to even them out. Do not try to make or clean up any incised lines after the concrete starts to harden; it may damage or crumble the stone. If you must, wait until 48 hours have passed and go over your lines with the tip of a bent paper clip. This is still risky because chipping or flaking is possible.

20 ➤ Set the stone aside to harden for 48 hours. Use the board to set the stone aside to cure for 48 hours. Cover the stone loosely with plastic and spray it with water after 24 hours.

21 ➤ Clean up the stone. After 48 hours, follow the directions on page 39 to clean the stone.

22 ➤ Elevate the stone and let it cure. Let the stone cure, elevated on a rack or on pencils, for five more days. Cover it loosely with plastic so that it cures slowly, which makes a sturdier stone. Spray it with water every 24 hours. After five days, the stone will be ready for use, as long as no pressure is applied to it for an additional seven days.

To enlarge these patterns
for a 12" (30cm) mold, use
a copy machine to enlarge
them 200%.

Petroglyph ➤

I like the simplicity of this bowl-shaped sheep. The tesserae are fragments from other projects. You can create your own combination of leftover bits and pieces from your projects. This project will further explore the technque of incising lines to add detail to a mosaic.

In keeping with the origin and spirit of the image, I added terra-cotta pigment to the mix. If this appeals to you, I recommend exploring Aboriginal art, prehistoric cave paintings, and Native American pottery and sand paintings.

For a variation of this project, you could make a sand-cast mold, shaped and carved to look like a red rock fragment. Pack wet sand or dirt into a box, dig out a shape, pour in the wet mix and embed your tesserae.

MATERIALS

round stepping stone mold
12" x 1½" (30cm x 38mm)

pencil with eraser

scissors

craft knife

stained glass tesserae (mostly iridescent, rippled glass): light and dark teal green, dark aqua, light and dark amber, light lavender and light blue

rigid board

dust mask

rubber gloves

7 lbs. (3.2kg)
stepping stone concrete mix

2 oz. (58g) packet
terra-cotta colored dry pigment

mixing bowl

mixing tool

2 cups (472ml) water

3" (75mm) putty knife

optional: craft stick or writing tool, tweezers, ruler

1 ➤ Enlarge the Pattern. Use a copy machine to enlarge the petroglyph pattern on page 71. For this design it would be easier to make an extra copy of the pattern to use as the Design Template than to use the cut-out parts from the Mold Template.

2 ➤ Make the templates. Place the mold on the paper template, centering it over the design. Trace the mold with a pencil then cut along the line. Use a craft knife to cut out the figure to make your Mold Template. You can choose how much detail to cut out; I cut out every detail, but you could cut out only the largest figure. Then after embedding the tesserae for the large sheep and removing the template, you would approximate the position of the two small figures and the spiral line.

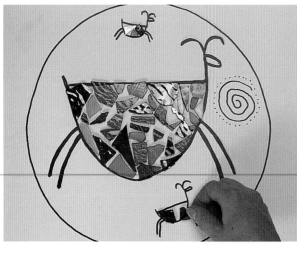

3 ➤ Arrange tesserae on the Design Template. First place the key pieces, which are the two upper corners of the figure. Then outline along the top with long straight-edged pieces, and along the belly with slightly curved pieces. Finally, fill in the figure. Alternate sizes, colors and shapes of glass pieces. Put just one or two pieces in each of the two tiny figures.

4 ➤ Prepare the mold and the mix. Place the mold on a board. Put on a dust mask and gloves and prepare the mix as described on pages 23-26. If you want to add colorant, follow the directions on page 27. Check the time or set a timer for one hour. If you haven't incised lines, see the "tip" below.

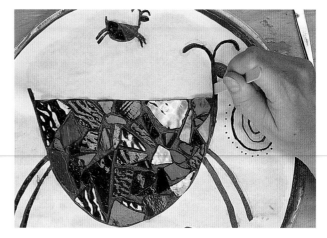

5 ➤ Place the Mold Template on the wet mix surface. Be sure the design is centered in the mold.

6 ➤ Transfer all tesserae. Transfer the tesserae in the same order you placed them on the Design Template: key pieces, outline, then fill in. Do not embed them yet. If you keep the pieces inside the cut paper edge, it will make removing the template much easier.

7 ➤ Incise the lines. If you did not cut out the lines for the legs and antlers, you must remove the template for this step. Otherwise, use the cut-out lines for positioning the incised lines. Follow the template lines with a craft stick, pencil, or toothpick. Use an up-and-down motion to incise dots or lines. Keep them ⅛" (3mm) away from the edge of the glass. Don't try to make perfect or deep lines yet.

tip

If this is your first time incising lines, practice making lines immediately after smoothing the mix in the mold. When you are finished practicing, re-smooth and jiggle the mold until all the marks have disappeared.

8 ➤ Remove the template. If you haven't done this already, slowly peel off the paper template. Some glass pieces may overlap the paper. If so, carefully lift the paper around them. Stand back and squint to see if any adjustments are needed. If so, do it now.

9 ➤ Embed the glass. When you have all the pieces placed, begin embedding them. Push straight down. Be sure that the outline pieces don't shift.

10 ➤ Jiggle the mold. Gently jiggle the mold now, smoothing and leveling the tesserae and the surface as described on page 35. The lines will fill in a bit, and you should stop before they disappear. After you make the final outlines and marks, don't jiggle the mold at all or the lines will disappear.

11 ➤ Incise the lines again. Go over all the rough lines you made earlier and add any others you would like, pushing the tool about ¼" (6mm) into the mix and using a dabbing motion. Again, keep the outline ⅛" (3mm) away from the glass. The lines should look dry and crisp. If the lines are soggy or fill in with water, wait ten minutes and try again. You may need to go over the lines two or three times. Make the border of dots around the spiral with a pointed tool.

Do not try to make or clean up any incised lines after the one-hour time limit is up—it may damage or crumble the stone. If you need to do this, wait 48 hours and use the tip of a bent paper clip. This is still risky; chipping or flaking is very possible.

12 ➤ Add the border. If the hour is not yet up, make the border impressions. Hold the stick at a 45° angle and make a shallow impression every 1" to 1½" (25mm to 38mm) about ½" (12mm) from the edge of the stone.

13 ➤ Set the stone aside to harden. Do not smooth or jiggle the mold. Set your stone aside to harden for 48 hours; spray it with water after 24 hours.

14 ➤ Clean up the stone. After 48 hours, follow the directions on page 39 to clean up the stone. Rinse it well.

15 ➤ Elevate the stone and let it cure. Follow directions on page 40 for this step. After five days the stone will be ready, if no pressure is applied to it for seven more days.

Frog Wall Stone

➤ This beautiful, multihued teal green glass is sold in a pet supply stores as aquarium gravel. It's an assortment of recycled and tumbled "chunky" glass: odds and ends, some curved, some flat, some lumps and chunks. Notice how the glass color changes when it's put on a gray concrete background: bright colors dim to midrange, and midrange colors fade almost to black. That's due to the translucency of this glass. Conversely, opaque glass is not affected by the color of the bedding material. Craft stores carry "sea glass," which is tumbled recycled glass that comes in both translucent and opaque colors. Beachcombers can find real sea glass washed up on the shore.

Variations of this project include using flat glass, which makes this an easier project. Also, since frogs come in shades of brown (or are those toads?) you can substitute highly polished rocks for the glass.

MATERIALS

square stepping stone mold
12" x 12" x 1½"
(30cm x 30cm x 38mm)

pencil with eraser

scissors

craft knife

teal green chunky glass
(I used Seaglass brand aquarium glass)

4 teal green vitreous glass tiles,
¾" x ¾" (2cm x 2cm)

1 black glass marble

rigid board

mounting device:
2"x 2" (5cm x 5cm) cardboard square,
3"x 2" (8cm x 5cm) piece of duct tape

dust mask

rubber gloves

7 lbs. (3.2kg)
stepping stone concrete mix

mixing bowl

mixing tool

2 cups (472ml) water

3" (75mm) putty knife

1 ➤ Enlarge the pattern. Use a copy machine to enlarge the frog pattern on page 81. For a 12" (30cm) mold, enlarge it 125%.

2 ➤ Make the templates. Place your mold on the enlarged pattern, centering it over the design. Trace the mold with a pencil. Use scissors to cut on the line. Use a craft knife to cut out the frog. This is your Mold Template. Use the cut-out frog or an extra enlarged pattern for your Design Template.

3 ➤ Sort the tesserae. The glass used in this project is not all one thickness; it is chunky, curved, thick and thin. Sorting this chunky type of glass by size will make it easier for you to find just the right piece. And since the frog is almost symmetrical, look for matching pairs of tesserae while you're sorting.

4 ➤ Lay out key pieces. Start by laying out the key pieces on the Design Template. Find pieces for the four feet; then find pieces about the size of corn kernels for the toe tips. Next find three pairs of matching tesserae for the six joints. Take time to find shapes that match the bend of the joints. Finally, finish filling in the legs.

5 ➤ Complete the outline and fill in the frog. Outline and fill in the rest of the figure.

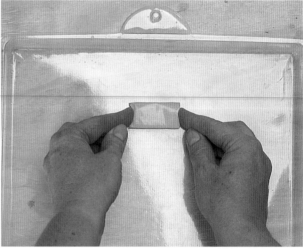

6 ➤ Prepare the mold with a mounting device. If your frog is to be a wall plaque, refer to page 21 for instructions on making an indentation on the back to accommodate a nail or screw.

7 ➤ Prepare the mix. Place the mold on a board. Put on a dust mask and gloves and prepare the mix as described on pages 23-26. Check the time or set a timer for one hour.

tip

If you use chunky glass, try to keep the glass clean as you work, and do not use a sponge to smooth the surface at the end. These two tips will save you lots of time when you clean up your stone later.

8 ➤ Transfer the tesserae. Position the Mold Template on the wet mix surface and smooth it down. Transfer the tesserae in the same order as you laid them out: first the feet, joints, and legs.

9 ➤ Embed the tesserae (optional). As you become more confident working with mosaics and concrete, you may want to embed the pieces as you arrange them on the mix.

10 ➤ Finish layout on the mix. Finish laying out the rest of the figure on the mix surface. Fill in the limbs, outline the figure, and fill in the rest of the body. Finally, embed the marble eye.

11 ➤ Finish embedding. Make adjustments if necessary, and embed the rest of the pieces. Embed the pieces with the template still in place so you can follow the outline more easily. After embedding, you can still add a couple of pieces to fill in any spaces. Carefully peel away the template. If any glass pieces overlap the paper, carefully lift the paper around them.

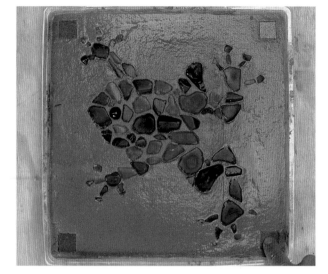 

12 ➤ Add the border pieces. Position and embed the square tiles in the corners, about ¼" to ½" (6mm to 10mm) in from the edges.

13 ➤ Jiggle the mold. Gently jiggle the mold now, smoothing and leveling the surface. When the tesserae are very irregular and lumpy, don't sponge the surface. Cleaning the stone later would be very time-consuming, because you would have to scrape and uncover almost every mosaic piece.

14 ➤ Set the stone aside to harden for 48 hours. Cover the stone loosely with plastic and use the board to pick it up to set aside for 48 hours. Spray with water after 24 hours.

15 ➤ Clean up the stone. After 48 hours, follow the directions page 39 for cleaning and unmolding. Rinse well.

16 ➤ Elevate the stone and let it cure. Let the stone cure, elevated on a rack or on pencils, for five more days. Cover it loosely with plastic so that it cures slowly, making a sturdier stone. Spray it with water every 24 hours. After five days the stone will be ready for use, as long as no pressure is applied to it for an additional seven days.

To enlarge this pattern for a 12" (30cm) mold,
use a copy machine to enlarge it 125%.

Fleur de Lis Tabletop

The fleur de lis, or "flower of the lily," has many symbolic meanings, among them purity, the Holy Trinity and the royal badge of France. It is a very elegant and simple design. In this project the entire surface is covered with tesserae. Because the table legs required a tabletop 15½" (40cm) across, this is the largest project in the book. Any of the designs in this book could be enlarged to this scale. When you make a large project, you must plan carefully, work quickly after filling the mold with mix and keep a close eye on the time. The mold I used was a deli tray lid from the grocery store. The scalloped edge provides a decorative touch.

This project uses two new mosaic materials, ceramic tile and smalti. Although smalti is expensive, it is well worth adding a few pieces to the background for extra sparkle (see page 10 for more about smalti). Broken or unglazed ceramic tile pieces are easier to push into the mix if they're soaked in water beforehand. Ceramic often breaks unevenly and the broken edges may have over- or underhangs that interfere with placing two pieces close to one another. If you haven't worked with ceramic tile before, try a smaller project first or practice embedding a few pieces after preparing the mix.

The timeless fleur de lis lends itself to many variations. You might make a smaller version and add a wall mount for hanging, or make a series of fleur de lis stepping stones with either solid or multicolored backgrounds. The white fleur de lis could be made from broken white china or even white pebbles.

MATERIALS

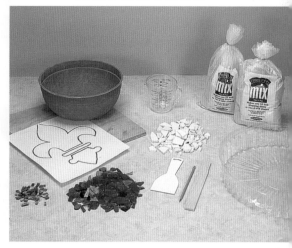

large round mold
(I used a plastic party tray lid with a fluted edge, 15½" x 2" or 40cm x 5cm)

pencil with eraser

scissors

craft knife

small bowl of water for soaking the tile

broken white ceramic tile

translucent stained glass in assorted blues and blue-greens

assorted gold smalti

rigid board

dust mask

rubber gloves

14 lbs. (6.4kg)
stepping stone concrete mix

mixing bowl

mixing tool

about 4 cups (945ml) water

3" (75mm) putty knife

small covered plastic dish

sponge and bowl of water

embedding block

optional: tweezers or craft stick

1 ➤ Enlarge the pattern. Use a copy machine to make two copies of the pattern on page 85 to fit your mold. You may have to make enlargements of two halves of the pattern, then tape them together.

2 ➤ Make the templates. One enlarged pattern should be on paper large enough to trace the entire mold for your Design Template. Trace the bottom of your mold onto the other enlarged pattern and use scissors to cut it out on the line (it doesn't have to be the whole outline). Use a craft knife to cut out the fleur de lis shape. This will be your Mold Template.

3 ➤ Soak the tile. Porous materials are easier to push into the mix if you briefly soak them in water. Either soak all the pieces at once and then do your layout, or soak each piece as you go. Wipe excess water from the pieces before laying them on the mix, because the water may leave a white powdery stain on the concrete that's hard to remove.

4 ➤ Arrange the white pieces on the design template.
Arrange the pieces on the template starting with the points, corners, and rounded ends. Then fill in the horizontal band and outline the upper and lower fleur de lis. Try to follow the flow of the curves. Using several smaller pieces will make this easier than using one or two large pieces. Finish by filling in the entire design.

5 ➤ Outline the design and fill in the background. Place blue glass around the outline of the fleur de lis shape. Start with corners, tight curves, points and narrow spaces. Next, place pieces for the outside edge, following the gentle curve and staying ½" (1cm) from the edge. Maintain a consistent space between the tesserae, about ¼" (6mm).

Then fill in the background with blue glass and gold pieces. The gold smalti usually are used gold side up, but are beautiful with the gold side down as well.

6 ➤ Prepare the mold and the mix. Due to the large mold, you may want to mix the concrete in two batches. Place the mold on a large, rigid board. Put on a dust mask and gloves and prepare the mix as described on pages 23-26. Set aside some mix in a covered plastic container for later. Empty the first batch in the mold, then mix and add the second batch on top of it. Tamp it well with your putty knife.

Check the time. This is a large stone and you will be covering the entire surface, so the process may take longer than with other projects. The mix will harden after an hour, as usual.

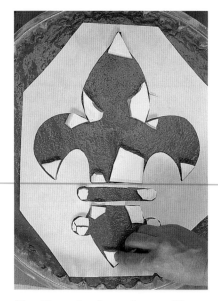

7 ➤ Transfer key pieces. Place the Mold Template on the wet mix surface and transfer the pieces in the same order as you laid them out: first the points, corners and rounded ends. Don't embed yet.

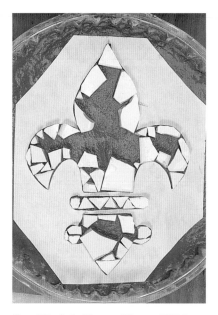

8 ➤ Finish the outline. Fill in the horizontal band and outline the upper and lower fleur de lis, following the flow of the curves. Finish filling in the entire fleur de lis. Be careful to keep pieces inside the paper edge.

9 ➤ Peel off the template.
Carefully peel away the template and check to see that the outline is smooth and symmetrical. You may see a few gray spaces that need filling in with tile. Add those pieces now.

10 ➤ Embed the tile. Begin by using your fingers to partially push in all the tile pieces, especially the large ones. Be careful that the outline pieces don't shift as you push them in.

Next, use the block to evenly embed all the tile pieces. I prefer to use the embedding block method here for two reasons: First, tile can be difficult to push into the mix because it absorbs water from the mix; and second, the block will evenly embed all the pieces, making a smooth surface and covering up sharp tile edges.

11 ➤ Fill depressions. All tile edges should be submerged in the mix. Use a craft stick and the mix that you set aside to fill in areas that need more concrete. It's OK to get wet mix on the tile surface; you can clean it up later.

12 ➤ Transfer the background pieces. Check your time. It may be getting difficult to push in the pieces, so work quickly!

Next, outline the entire fleur de lis shape with the blue glass. Transfer the glass from your Design Template starting with corners, tight curves, points and narrow spaces. Then outline the mold with blue glass, following the gentle curve and staying ½" (1cm) from the edge.

13 ➤ Fill in the background. Fill in the background with blue and gold glass. When you're satisfied with the arrangement, embed the pieces using an embedding block or your fingertips. Embed any small filler pieces with a pencil eraser tip.

14 ➤ Jiggle the mold. Gently jiggle the mold or tap the sides, leveling and smoothing the surface and pieces as described on page 35. This may take some time on such a large stone. Look closely from several angles to be sure every piece is well-embedded and the surface is smooth, especially if this is to be a tabletop. Wipe the surface with a sponge, concentrating on the areas with tile.

15 ➤ Set the stone aside to harden for 48 hours. Cover the stone loosely with plastic and use the board to transfer it to a safe location. Spray it with water after 24 hours.

16 ➤ Clean up the stone. After 48 hours, gently scrub excess concrete from the tesserae. Remove the stone from the mold and carefully round off the edges. Be very careful scraping the fluted edge — it will chip easily. Rinse the stone well.

17 ➤ Elevate the stone and let it cure. Let the stone cure, elevated on a rack or on pencils, for five more days, spraying it with water every day. Cover it loosely with plastic, making a sturdier stone. After five days the stone will be ready for use, as long as no pressure is applied to it for seven more days.

To enlarge this pattern for a 15½" (40cm) mold, use a copy machine to enlarge it 200% then enlarge the copy 125%.

Garden Gloves

➤ This stepping stone was created in the spirit of a **trompe l'oeil,** or "trick the eye" painting in which three-dimensional objects are realistically depicted on a flat surface. I doubt anyone will bend down to try and pick up these gloves, but they would add a lighthearted touch to a garden path, landscaping or porch.

You could make a path of plain gray concrete stepping stones and place this one in the middle. The glove motif would look clever as a small round tabletop for a sunroom that has lots of plants. You could add a border of pebbles or random shapes of mosaic glass. For an easier version of this design, join and round off the fingers to make a pair of colorful mittens.

MATERIALS

square stepping stone mold
12" x 12" x 2" (30cm x 30cm x 5cm)

pencil with eraser

scissors

craft knife

opaque white and translucent
dark blue stained glass

rigid board

dust mask

rubber gloves

7 lbs (3.2kg)
stepping stone concrete mix

mixing bowl

mixing tool

2 cups (472ml) water

3" (75mm) putty knife

optional: tweezers

1 ➤ **Enlarge the pattern.** Use a copy machine to enlarge the garden gloves pattern on page 89. Make three copies.

2 ➤ **Make the templates.** Place the mold on one enlarged pattern, centering it over the design. Trace the mold with a pencil. Use scissors to cut out along the traced line to make the Mold Template. Repeat for a second Mold Template. Use a craft knife to cut out just the white gloves from one Mold Template. Then cut out just the blue wristbands from the other Mold Template. The third copy can be your Design Template.

3 ➤ **Lay out white tesserae on the template.** Arrange the white glass on the Design Template starting with the ten fingers. Look for pieces with rounded edges which will follow the tight curves of the narrow, elongated fingers. Tiny pieces and careful fitting are required. Fairly tight spacing will ensure that the image "reads" easily.

Next, place a white piece in each of the three corners, adjacent to the wristbands. Then outline the rest of the hand, staying within the line, and finish by filling it in.

4 ➤ Lay out blue tesserae on the template. Now arrange the dark blue pieces of the wristbands. Begin with the four corners of the top glove (the right hand). Next, place the outline pieces. Then fill in the center.

Lay out the other band: place the three corners, outline and fill in. If you follow this order, the illusion of one glove lying on top of the other will be more apparent.

5 ➤ Prepare the mold and the mix. Place the mold on a board. Prepare the mix as described on pages 23-26. Place the white gloves Mold Template on the wet mix surface. Check the time or set a timer for one hour.

6 ➤ Transfer the tesserae. Start transferring the white tesserae for the hands, starting with the key white pieces. Keep the spacing even and fairly tight, about ⅛" (3mm). Let the pieces just rest on the surface for now.

7 ➤ Finish the hands. Outline and fill in the hands. Use tweezers to insert small pieces and adjust others. Be careful to keep the pieces inside the open space in the template.

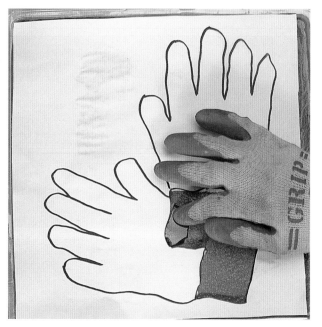

8 ➤ Switch templates and transfer tesserae. Carefully remove the glove template and place the wristband template on the mix. Next, position the blue pieces of the top glove.

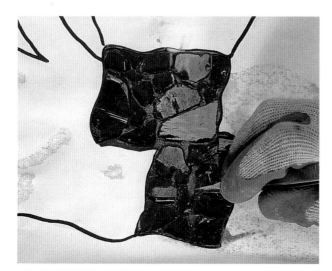

9 ➤ Finish the bands. Transfer the pieces for the bottom glove, placing the corners and outline first. Then fill in and adjust the spacing if necessary.

10 ➤ Embed the tesserae. Carefully peel away the template, then stand back and look at the layout. Does the outline of the entire shape look like a pair of baggy cotton gloves? The pieces should be evenly and tightly spaced, with room for mix to come up between them when you push down. The four fingers of each glove should be close to each other, with a V-shaped space between them. If you see a few gray spaces that still need filling in, add those pieces now.

When you have all the pieces where you want them, begin embedding. Push straight down.

11 ➤ Jiggle the mold. Gently jiggle the mold, leveling and smoothing the surface and pieces as described on page 35.

12 ➤ Set the stone aside to harden for 48 hours. Cover the stone loosely with plastic and use the board to transfer it to a safe location. Spray it with water after 24 hours.

13 ➤ Clean up the stone. After 48 hours, gently scrub the excess concrete from the tesserae as described on page 39. Remove stone from the mold and round off the edges as shown on page 39. Rinse the stone well.

14 ➤ Elevate the stone and let it cure. Let the stone cure elevated on a rack or on pencils for five more days. Cover it loosely with plastic to cure more slowly, which makes a sturdier stone. Spray it with water every 24 hours. After five days the stone will be ready for use, as long as no pressure is applied to it for an additional seven days.

To enlarge this pattern for a 12 " (30cm) mold, use a copy machine to enlarge it 200%, then enlarge the copy 130%.

House Number Sign

➤ This house number sign can be made as a wall plaque that hangs on your house or garage, or it can be embedded in a curbside garden. The main consideration here is legibility; in order for the numbers to "read," keep the spacing between the pieces tight, ⅛" (3mm) maximum. This mold will easily fit two to four numerals; if your address is longer, you could build your own mold or buy a longer mold. You could make this project easier by leaving out the background mosaic pieces, but be sure to use a glass color that reads well against the concrete color. Opaque glass is best for legibility because translucent glass tends to fade into the gray concrete background. I chose blue and orange, which are complementary colors and provide a good contrast. You could also choose black and white, a bright color on a white background, yellow on blue or any other contrasty combination. If you can easily distinguish between the two colors when you squint your eyes, you have a good contrast.

Another idea would be to make this a yard sign by inserting two metal stakes, an inch from each end, through the bottom edge of the mold. (See page 121, Garden Stakes and Paperweights.) Use an awl to punch the holes in the plastic mold.

MATERIALS

house sign mold,
12" x 8" x 1" (30cm x 30cm x 25mm)

pencil with eraser

enlarged number patterns
11" x 17" (28cm x 43cm) paper

scissors

craft knife

ruler

clear tape

opaque light blue and
orange stained glass

optional: orange glass heart ornament

rigid board

optional mounting device:
2" x 2" (5cm x 5cm) cardboard square
3" x 2" (8cm x 5cm) piece of duct tape

dust mask

rubber gloves

3½ lbs. (1.6kg)
stepping stone concrete mix

mixing bowl

mixing tool

1 cup (236ml) water

3" (75mm) putty knife

sponge and small bowl of water

tweezers

optional: embedding block

1 ➤ Enlarge the pattern. Enlarge the numbers you need from page 95. For this mold, the numbers should be about 3 ⅛" (9cm) tall.

2 ➤ Make the templates. Trace your mold onto a sheet of paper and arrange the numbers so they are spaced about ⅜"(1cm) apart and are no closer than ⅛" to the edge of the mold. Tape down the numbers. This is your Design Template.

Make a photocopy or tracing of the Design Template. Cut with scissors along the outline of the mold; then use a craft knife to cut out the numbers. Numbers 4, 6, 8, 9, and 0 have holes, and you will need to cut out and save the inside part. This is your Mold Template.

3 ➤ Lay out the numerals on the template. Lay out your glass pieces on the Design Template, starting with the numbers. Carefully follow the tight corners, turns and curves. Look for small pieces with straight edges and curves that match the outlines of the numerals. The numbers will be easier to read if you keep the spacing tight.

4 ➤ Lay out the background on the template.
If you have a heart ornament, position it ⅜" (1cm)
from the top edge. Next, find background pieces that
fit into the numerals' negative spaces (a triangle for a **4**,
two round pieces for an **8**, etc.) and then fill in between
each numeral. Place pieces for the four mold corners.

Now outline the numerals. Again, take the time
to do a precise layout. Keep spacing fairly tight and
consistent.

Finally, outline the entire stone and fill it in. I like
to use a variety of sizes and shapes and really mix
them up. This makes a more interesting design.

5 ➤ Prepare the mounting device. If you want to
hang up your sign, you'll need a recessed area in the
back to accommodate a nail or screw. See page 21 for
the instructions for making this device.

6 ➤ Prepare the mix. Put on a dust mask and
gloves and follow pages 23-26 to prepare the mix.
Check the time; this project will take more time than
the others since the placement of glass is precise and
the entire stone surface is being covered.

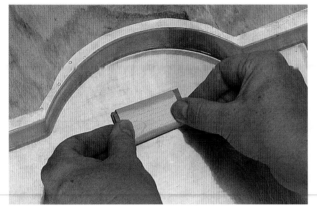

8 ➤ Transfer the numeral pieces. As quickly as
possible, transfer the numeral pieces to the mix surface. Keep the pieces inside the paper edge and let
them rest on top of the mix for the time being.

Remove the template and make sure the numbers
are legible, centered, and level with each other. Make
any adjustments and keep an eye on the time.

7 ➤ Place the template on the wet mix surface.
Place the Mold Template on the wet mix surface, then
carefully place the cut-out paper pieces to create the
negative spaces in the numbers that need them.
Tweezers are helpful here.

9 ➤ Embed the numerals.
If you embed the numerals now, they will stay in place as you position the background pieces. The pencil eraser head is especially good to push in these small pieces. Work rather quickly, being careful not to shift the pieces as you press them into the mix.

10 ➤ Position the key background pieces. Whether you embedded the numerals or not, now transfer the background pieces in the same order as above: first the heart ornament, numeral negative spaces and the four corners. Then outline the numerals and then the mold border, keeping pieces about ¼" (6mm) from the edge of the mold.

11 ➤ Fill in the background. Fill in the rest of the background. Place the last piece, stand back and take a good look. Move or add any pieces that seem necessary now.

12 ➤ Embed the background. When pieces are spaced this closely together I like to use the embedding block as described on page 31. You could embed the pieces with your finger or a pencil eraser instead.

Push the thickest piece in first, which is the heart. Then embed all the rest. Look for gray spaces that still may need a piece of glass. Add those pieces.

13 ➤ Jiggle the mold and sponge the surface. Gently jiggle the mold, leveling the pieces and smoothing the surface. Sponging the surface will be very helpful after using an embedding block. See page 35.

14 ➤ Set the stone aside to harden for 48 hours. Cover the stone loosely with plastic and use the board to transfer it to a safe location. Spray it with water after 24 hours.

15 ➤ Clean up the stone. After 48 hours, gently scrub the excess concrete from the tesserae as described on page 39. Remove the stone from the mold and round off the edges as shown on page 39. Rinse the stone well.

16 ➤ Elevate the stone and let it cure. Let the stone cure, elevated on a rack or on pencils, for five more days. Cover it loosely with plastic so that it cures slowly, which makes a sturdier stone. Spray it with water every 24 hours. After five days the stone will be ready for use.

t i p

The contact-paper technique described on pages 32-34 could also be used for this project. Arrange just the numerals on the Design Template. Adhere the contact paper to the numerals, transfer them to the mix and embed them, then remove the contact paper within about five minutes. Then arrange the background pieces and embed them as explained in the project above.

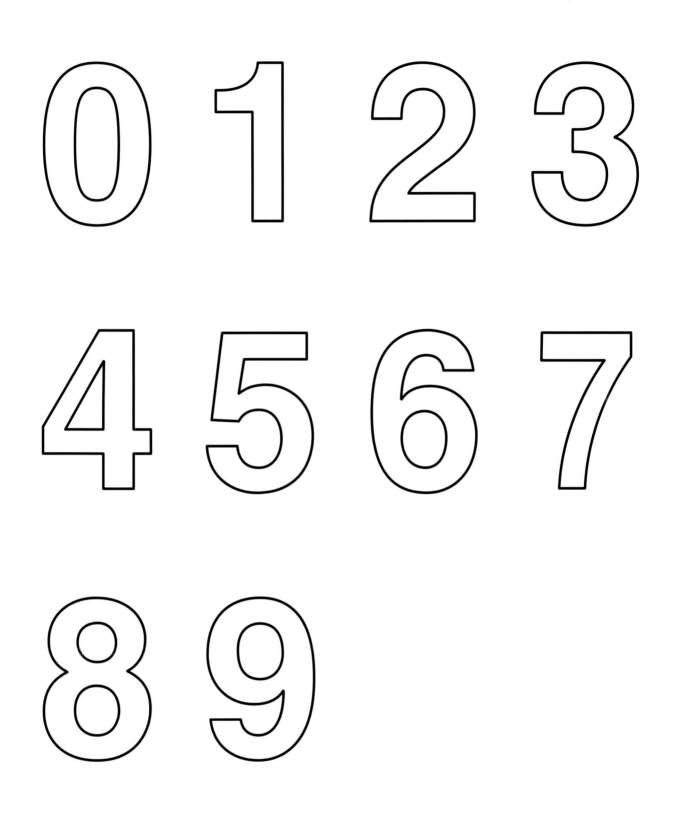

To enlarge these numbers for a 12" x 8"
(30cm x 20cm) mold, use a copy machine to
enlarge them 200%.

Lizard

➤ A shiny black reptile and highly polished black rocks are a match made in mosaic heaven! Take your time laying out this project. It's important to find stone shapes that flow into one another, and that smoothly graduate in size from the broad head and shoulders to the pointed tail tip. Laying out a design which includes river rocks, broken plates, marbles, or other irregularly shaped pieces can be frustrating—the pieces tip over, roll off the table and just generally don't stay put. I solve this problem by using a shallow box of sand for laying out the design. The dry sand holds uneven pieces in place no matter which way they are placed.

For variations of this project, think about using different rock colors: dark green, terra-cotta red, even off-white. This design may be made of glass tesserae so you can give your lizard's tail colorful contrasting stripes using the glass on edge. If you plan to use this lizard for a garden path, flip the design over and trace it from the back; then alternate the patterns so your lizards slither one way and then the other as the path unfolds.

MATERIALS

square stepping stone mold
12" x 12" x 1½"
(30cm x 30cm x 38mm)

pencil with eraser

scissors

craft knife

optional: sand in a shallow box or tray

about 50 polished black river rocks,
grape-to plum-size

rigid board

dust mask

rubber gloves

7 lbs. (3.2kg)
stepping stone concrete mix

mixing bowl

mixing tool

2 cups (472ml) water

3" (75mm) putty knife

tweezers

embedding block

1 ➤ Enlarge the pattern. Use a copy machine to enlarge the lizard pattern on page 101 to fit the size of your mold. Make two copies.

2 ➤ Make the templates. Place the mold on one enlarged pattern, centering it over the design. Trace the mold with a pencil and cut on the line with scissors. Use a craft knife to cut out the lizard. This is the Mold Template, and if you're using a tray of sand to lay out your pieces, it is the only template you will need. Otherwise, use another copy of the enlarged pattern or the cut-out lizard as your Design Template.

3 ➤ Sort the rocks. First sort the river rocks by size. This will make finding just the right piece much quicker. Try to use flat rocks, not thick, rounded ones that might contact the bottom of the mold when embedded.

4 ➤ Lay out the head, body and tail. If you're using a sand tray, lay the Mold Template on the sand surface. If you prefer, you may instead lay out the rocks on the Design Template; the process is the same.

First make a curving snake figure that is like a backward *S* using twelve to sixteen rocks. Take time to play around with shapes and sizes and to find rocks that fit together well. The first three or four rocks need to touch the design outlines in order to define the smooth upper body curve. When you have an arrangement you like, look at it with squinted eyes to see that you have created a smooth curve. Line up the rocks as closely as possible to the paper template outline without overlapping the edge. If the rocks you have are small, you can make the body two rocks wide, but only between the front and back legs.

For the tail tip, find a flat rock that appears narrow when turned on its side. A good tail tip piece curves and comes to a slight point.

5 ➤ Lay out the legs. The four legs are almost identical: two parts with three or four toes each. Try to find pairs of rocks that match in size and shape. If your bag of rocks did not include rocks small enough for the toes, use the technique on pages 12-13 to smash a few rocks in half.

Remove the template, stand back and squint. Does the shape look like a backward *S* with smooth bends and no kinks? Rearrange the pieces until your lizard looks as if it will slither away.

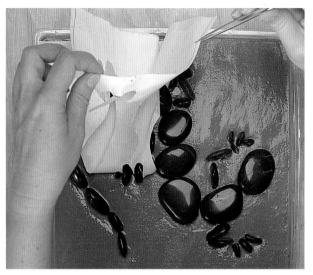

6 ➤ Prepare the mold and the mix. Place the mold on a board. Put on your dust mask and gloves to prepare the mix as described on pages 23-26. Check the time or set a timer for 60 minutes.

7 ➤ Transfer the rocks. Position the Mold Template on the wet mix surface and smooth it down.

Quickly move the rocks to the mix surface, beginning with the head and working down the figure to the tail tip. Then transfer the pieces for the legs and toes. Space the rocks so that they touch. Don't push the rocks in the mix yet; however, you can partially embed broken pieces just enough to keep them in place. Use tweezers to position smaller pieces.

8 ➤ Remove the template. Slowly peel off the paper template. If some rocks overlap the paper, carefully lift the paper around them. Stand back to see if any adjustments are needed. If so, do it now.

9 ➤ Push in the rocks. Rocks are sometimes difficult to push straight down into the mix, even if the concrete hasn't begun to harden. Try to gently seesaw or vibrate the rock while pushing down. Push the rocks in at least three-fourths of the way. Don't push them in too far, or you'll end up with a chain of small "icebergs," the visible portion of the rocks having shrunk while most of the bulk disappears into the mix. Push each piece in, then go back and do it again until all rocks are properly embedded.

If you find that water is pooling around the rocks, soak up the excess with a paper towel.

If you want a more level surface, use a weighted block after you have partially embedded the rocks with your fingers, as shown on page 31. This will level the peaks of the rocks. You may choose to embed the rocks completely so that they are flush with the surface of the stone. This surface is better for walking on, but the rocks tend to lose some detail and the space between them grows larger. I prefer to just push in the rocks as in step 9 and just enjoy the bumpy surface of the stepping stone.

10 ➤ Patch valleys. When you've finished embedding, you may see a few small valleys or depressions surrounding some of the rocks. You may choose to leave them alone (which would be my choice), or you may fill them in with wet concrete as described on page 43. Keep in mind that if you fill in the valleys or sponge the surface, the rocks will lose some detail and the spacing will not look as tight as before.

11 ➤ Smooth the mix and jiggle the mold. If you want a very smooth surface, use the putty knife lightly to even out the surface texture. Gently jiggle the mold.

12 ➤ Set the stone aside to harden for 48 hours. Cover the stone loosely with plastic and use the board to transfer it to a safe location. Spray with water after 24 hours.

13 ➤ Clean up the stone. After 48 hours, gently scrub excess concrete from the rocks as described on page 38. Remove the stone from the mold and round off the edges as shown on page 39. Rinse the stone.

14 ➤ Elevate the stone and let it cure. Let the stone cure, elevated on a rack or on pencils, for five more days. Cover it loosely with plastic so that it cures slowly, which makes a sturdier stone. Spray it with water every 24 hours. When the five days are up, your stone is ready to be used as long as no pressure is applied to it for an additional seven days.

To enlarge these patterns for a 12" (30cm) mold, use a copy machine to enlarge them 200%.

Pot of Geraniums

> The next four projects include some very large "tesserae": a terra-cotta pot, a pair of scrub brushes, a teacup and a plant hook. Even for the experienced mosaic artist, these objects can be tricky to handle and awkward to embed, so take your time planning and laying out these designs. Read through the steps until you have a clear idea of what you'll need to do and in what order.

This wall plaque is a bit whimsical, because the mosaic flowers "grow" out of the three-dimensional pot. The pot has no real function, although you could keep your garden tools or keys in it. If the plaque is hanging on a sunny porch, you could add soil and flower seeds and see what happens, but I prefer just to leave it as it is.

You may come up with other ways to incorporate embedded containers into your mosaic projects.. You can cut a small tin pail in half with tin snips and use it in place of the pot. And of course, you can use different colors and substitute daisies or other kinds of flowers for the geraniums.

MATERIALS

hacksaw

4" (10cm) terra-cotta pot

square stepping stone mold
12" x 12" x 1½"
(30cm x 30cm x 38mm)

pencil with eraser

scissors

craft knife

translucent orange and frosted dark
green stained glass pieces

rigid board

mounting device:
2"x 2" (5cm x 5cm) cardboard square
3"x 2" (8cm x 5cm) piece of duct tape

dust mask

rubber gloves

7 lbs. (3.2kg)
stepping stone concrete mix

mixing bowl

mixing tool

2 cups (472ml) water

3" (75mm) putty knife

tweezers

1 ➤ Saw the pot in half. Use a hacksaw to cut the pot in half vertically. Don't worry about being too precise. The easiest way to do this is to cut halfway down, then turn the pot over and cut down until the second cut joins the first.

2 ➤ Enlarge the pattern. Use a copy machine to enlarge the geranium pattern on page 101 to fit your mold. For a 12" (30cm) square mold, enlarge it 200%. Make two copies of the pattern.

3 ➤ Make the templates. Place the mold on the enlarged pattern, centering it over the design. Trace the mold with a pencil. Use scissors to cut out along the traced line. Use a craft knife to cut out the flowers and leaves, but not the stems or the pot outline. This is the Mold Template; use the other enlarged pattern for the Design Template.

4 ➤ Lay out tesserae on the Design Template. You'll need about 45 orange petal pieces that are similar in size and shape: oval or elongated, about the size of small grapes. Arrange them on the Design Template starting with the flower outlines, then fill in the entire flower area.

Next arrange the green leaf pieces. Start with the key pieces located at the line where the leaves meet the pot rim. Outline these two

corners with green pieces. Place the half-pot on the template to serve as a guide. Next, outline the rest of the leaves, then fill them in. Stay well within the outlines.

Select twelve to fifteen small green stem pieces (glass pieces that will be set on their sides) and set them aside.

5 ➤ Prepare the mounting device. Prepare and position the cardboard and duct tape mounting device as shown on page 21. Since the mold is square, you may want to mark the top of the mold with a piece of tape.

6 ➤ Prepare the mix. Place the mold on a board. Put on your mask and gloves and prepare the mix as described on pages 22-26. Check the time or set a timer for one hour.

7 ➤ Transfer the flower pieces. Position the Mold Template on the wet mix surface. Transfer the flower pieces to the mix starting with the outlines. Fill in each flower with petals, spacing the pieces closely to resemble the flower petals.

8 ➤ Transfer the leaf pieces. Transfer the leaves to the mix surface, starting with the key pieces and the outlines; then fill them in.

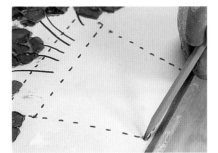

9 ➤ Mark the position of the pot. Test the placement of the half-pot now; place it on the template, lining it up with the top dotted line. Check to see if there is ½" to ¾" (12mm to 18mm) between the base of the pot and the edge of the stone. Also make sure that the pot fits between—not on top of—the two leaves. (If it doesn't, you can fix it in a moment.) Then remove the pot.

Use a pencil to make marks through the dotted lines at the four corners of the pot so that there are marks that will remain in the wet mix after the template has been removed.

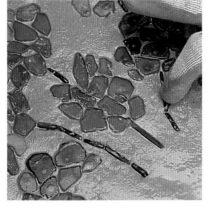

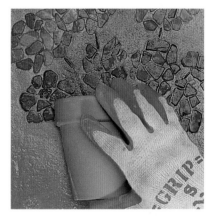

10 ➤ Embed the flower and leaf pieces. If any rearranging is needed to accommodate the pot, do it now. Then embed the flowers and leaves by pushing straight down or use an embedding block.

11 ➤ Remove the template. Before you make the stems, carefully remove the Mold Template.

12 ➤ Create the stems. Mark the position of the stems by drawing light guidelines or dots in the mix with the tip of a pencil. Then begin pushing in green pieces on their edges. Start at the base of a flower and work your way down the stem, going below the pot rim about 1" (25mm). Do this for both of the stems.

13 ➤ Embed the pot. Position the pot no less than ½" (12mm) from the edge. Embed the pot, rocking it gently while pushing down. You want it to go into the mix about 1" (25mm)—most of the way in but not all the way to the bottom. If it does go in too deeply, lift it up a little and jiggle the mold two or three times.

14 ➤ Tamp the mix. Using your gloved fingers, push the mix against the outer pot wall to firm the bond. Do this all around the pot, smoothing as you go.

15 ➤ Jiggle the mold. Gently jiggle and tap the sides of the mold to even out the surface, making sure the pot doesn't shift or sink all the way through the mix. For a more even texture, lightly skim the surface once with the putty knife.

16 ➤ Set the stone aside to harden. Cover the stone loosely with plastic and use the board to set it aside to harden for 48 hours. Spray it with water after 24 hours.

17 ➤ Clean up the stone. After 48 hours, gently scrub excess concrete from the tesserae as described on page 39. Remove the stone from the mold and remove the mounting device as shown on page 38; then round off the edges. Rinse the stone well.

18 ➤ Elevate the stone and let it cure. Let the stone cure, elevated on a rack or on pencils, for five more days. Cover it loosely with plastic so that it cures slowly, which makes a sturdier stone. Spray it with water every 24 hours. After five days the stone will be ready for use.

Pique Assiette Boot Brush

Pique assiette is a French term meaning "plate stealer," or scavenger. It refers to the folk art of using broken china and fragments of pottery to embellish everything from small items to entire houses. Many of these mosaics incorporate uncommon objects. I began with a colorful broken plate, then I selected some other broken tile and glass pieces that coordinated with the plate colors: deep purple, teal green, amber and light blue.

For a variation, you could use the same two brushes in a larger mold and add foot prints of your children and paw prints of your pets. You may want to add fewer mosaic pieces to allow for writing in the wet cement ("Please wipe," "The Smiths," your house number or "Welcome"). This project makes a clever gift for a friend who is tired of muddy shoes! If you use brushes with wooden handles, you should seal the wood first with two coats of acrylic paint.

MATERIALS

square stepping stone mold
12" x 12" x 1½"
(30cm x 30cm x 38mm)

pencil with eraser

paper

two 8"x 2" (20cm x 5cm)
scrub brushes with textured
plastic handles

ceramic plate, tile and glass bits
and pieces

small bowl of water for soaking tile

old towel

rigid board

dust mask

rubber gloves

7 lbs. (3.2kg)
stepping stone concrete mix

mixing bowl

mixing tool

2 cups (472ml) water

3" (75mm) putty knife

ruler

1 ➤ Soak broken ceramic pieces.
Read about working with ceramic
pieces before starting (see Getting
Started page 30). You may soak
broken ceramic pieces in water all
at once and then do your layout,
or soak each piece as you go. Wipe
each piece dry before placing it on
the template. Pre-soaked tiles are
easier to embed than dry ones, and
will create a smoother surface.

2 ➤ Make a template. If you
want to use a template, trace the
mold on a piece of paper; this will
be the only template. Place the two
brushes in the center of the traced
outline, about ⅜" (1cm) apart. Trace
a square around the brushes. Then
arrange mosaic pieces on the template, starting at the outline of the
brushes, staying ¼" (6mm) to ½"
(12mm) from the brushes. Next lay
the pieces for the outside edges,
and finally fill in the middle.

Your other option is to prepare
the mix, pour it into the mold and
simply start embedding without
laying out the pieces on the template first.

3 ➤ Prepare the mix. Place the
mold on a board. Put on a dust
mask and gloves and prepare the
mix as described on pages 23-26.
Check the time or set a timer for
one hour.

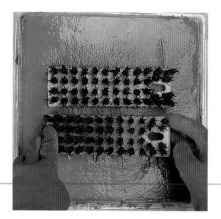

4 ➤ Position the brushes.
Position the brushes in the center
of the stone ⅜" (1cm) apart.

5 ➤ Embed the brushes. This
step will take a bit of muscle to
accomplish. Push straight down
on a brush and seesaw it from end
to end. Try vibrating it. It may be
hard to press in, but don't give
up. Then embed the other brush.
Make sure that the mix comes up
between the brushes and that the
mix is flush with the submerged
handles.

The law of mosaic embedding: "What goes
down, must come up." The mix will be signifi-
cantly displaced by the brushes so you'll notice rising mounds of mix around them.

6 ➤ Smooth the mix. Flatten
and smooth the mix with your
fingers. Be sure that the brush
handles are fully embedded and
that the mix comes up and over
their edges. Use a finger to smooth
the mix between the two brushes.
(It will be a little messy.) Then
smooth the surface with a putty
knife and give the mold a couple
of jiggles.

7 ➤ Position the mosaic pieces. Place the pieces beginning with the brush outline, then the mold corners and border, and then fill in the other areas. Be sure to stay ¼" (6mm) to ½" (12mm) from the brushes and the edge of the mold.

8 ➤ Embed the tesserae. If you're feeling confident, try embedding the pieces as you go. Otherwise, finish laying out all the pieces on the mix surface before pushing them all in.

Stand back and look at your design. If you see a few gray spaces or gaps that need to be filled in, add those pieces now. Check the level of the brushes because they tend to rise. Push the brushes in and level them if needed.

9 ➤ Fill in depressions. If you see any exposed irregular ceramic edges, use extra mix to fill these in now, as described on page 43.

10 ➤ Jiggle the mold and sponge the surface. Gently jiggle and turn the mold, leveling and smoothing the surface and pieces. Lightly sponge the surface.

11 ➤ Set the stone aside to harden. Cover the stone loosely with plastic and set it aside for 48 hours. Spray it with water after 24 hours.

12 ➤ Clean up the stone. After 48 hours, gently scrub excess concrete from the tesserae as described on page 39. Remove the stone from the mold and round off the edges. Rinse the stone well.

13 ➤ Elevate the stone and let it cure. Let the stone cure, elevated on a rack or on pencils, for five more days. Cover it loosely with plastic so that it cures slowly, which makes a sturdier stone. Spray it with water every 24 hours. After five days, uncover it and stop spraying it, but wait an additional seven days before using the boot brush.

tip

To hold your boot brush in place or to protect floors: After curing, cut a skid-resistant backing (such as a rubber mesh carpet pad) to match the stone shape. Glue it to the stone bottom with concrete glue or silicone-based glue.

Forget-Me-Not Wall Flower

> This project is so much fun! It includes an unexpected feature: a teacup which can hold a tiny potted plant, a bar of soap, or even tea bags. Your creation will be different from mine, but I hope I can inspire you to unpack old jewelry and uncover fun "junk" to include in your plaque. Arrange your design on a paper tracing of your mold, or design it as you go!

Other objects you could embed include: a small terra-cotta saucer as a bird feeder; a large hook to hang your hat; a ceramic soap dish to keep your keys or an antique saucer to hold a votive candle.

M A T E R I A L S

stepping stone mold
(I used a flower-shaped mold)
12" x 12" x 1½"
(30cm x 30cm x 38mm)

pencil with eraser

found objects: old jewelry, glass beads,
hardware, mirror and china pieces

smalti, broken tile and stained-glass

rigid board

mounting device:
2"x 2" (5cm x 5cm) cardboard square
3"x 2" (8cm x 5cm) piece of duct tape

dust mask

rubber gloves

7 lbs. (3.2kg)
stepping stone concrete mix

optional: two 2oz. (58g)
packets of charcoal-colored dry pigment

mixing bowl

mixing tool

2 cups (472ml) water

3" (75mm) putty knife

tweezers

1 ➤ Make a template if desired. If you want to plan your design, make a template by tracing your mold on a piece of paper. Arrange and rearrange your pieces on this template until you are happy with the design.

If you don't want to use a template, have your bits and pieces ready nearby. You will need to soak any broken ceramic pieces (see page 30).

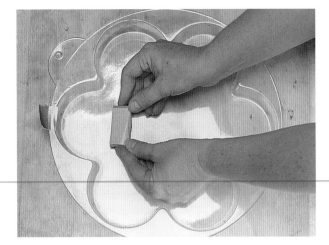

2 ➤ Prepare the mold for a mounting device.
See page 21 for directions on preparing a mold with
a hanging device.

3 ➤ Prepare the mix. If you want to color your
stone, see page 27 for directions on adding pigment to
the mix. Put your mold on a board, put on your dust
mask and gloves and follow the directions on pages
22-26 to prepare the mix. Check the time or set a timer
for one hour.

4 ➤ Position the cup. I started by placing a couple
of the larger and more important elements on the mix:
a sprocket from a bicycle and a faucet handle, which I
think of as the "flowers" of my design. Positioning
them first helped me choose the placement for the full-
size, unbroken teacup.

First, place the cup in the desired position and
gently push it into the mix, just enough to make an
impression.

5 ➤ Start embedding the cup.
Place the lip of the cup on the mark
and start to push it into the stone
at a 45° angle, 1" (25mm) deep. It's

similar to digging in the dirt with
a trowel: push the cup down and
away, then scoop and push it away
and up slightly, working to gently
loosen and lift the mix—but don't
shovel it out.

Keep scooping until a mound
of mix goes about halfway down
into the cup. Stop scooping and
push down on the bottom of the
cup. Vibrate and push the cup
gently to embed the bottom, then
straighten it out into its final
position. You'll probably have to
make several adjustments until
it's in the right place.

6 ➤ Secure the cup. Now the
cup needs to be bonded and secured
to the concrete. With a gloved
hand, push the mound of mix into
the cup, leveling it out as much as
possible, pressing it against the
cup and extending it all the way to
the bottom of the cup. Scoop a bit of
mix from elsewhere if needed.

t i p

If you are using broken china or broken ceramic tile, briefly soak the pieces in water

and wipe them dry before using them.

7 ➤ Make a shelf. Next, create a concrete shelf beneath the cup to add support. Scrape mix up against the bottom of the cup, forming a ledge underneath. With your fingertips, press around the entire seam where the cup and mix meet.

Optional: Gently, very gently, jiggle the mold to make an even, smooth surface.

8 ➤ Arrange and embed the tesserae. Try to work neatly from now on. You won't want to vibrate the mold after perfectly placing the teacup.

Position the rest of the pieces, keeping them about ¼" (6mm) from the edge. Rearrange them until you are satisfied, keeping an eye on the time. Then start pushing them into the mix, beginning with the thickest pieces and ending with the thinnest. Push straight down; seesaw and vibrate the larger pieces. Very thin, flat pieces, such as bicycle parts or coins, must be pushed in deeply so they will stay in place when the stone has cured.

When you've finished embedding, stand back and look at the stone. Fill in any spaces. Check the thin pieces again to ensure that they are flush with the surface, or even lower.

9 ➤ Smooth the surface. Tap the sides of the mold to even out the surface, but don't vibrate too hard or the heavier pieces may sink out of sight.

10 ➤ Set the stone aside to harden for 48 hours. Use the board to move the stone to a safe location. Cover it loosely with plastic and spray it with water after 24 hours.

11 ➤ Clean up the stone. After 48 hours, gently scrub excess concrete from the tesserae as described on page 39. Remove the stone from the mold, take out the duct tape and cardboard mounting device and round off the edges. Rinse the stone well.

12 ➤ Elevate the stone and let it cure. Let the stone cure, elevated on a rack or on pencils, for five more days. Cover it loosely with plastic so that it cures slowly, which makes a sturdier stone. Spray it with water every 24 hours. After five days the stone will be ready for use.

Sundial

> This sundial is designed for decorative purposes, not to tell the time right down to the minute. In order for a sundial to tell accurate time, it must be designed for the latitude and longitude of the place where it will be used. For more detailed information, look up sundials at your local library or on the Internet. The latitude of your city determines the spacing of the numbers and the angle of your pointer, or gnomon. The gnomon I used is actually an iron plant hook. You may use a different object such as a metal plant stake or a bent metal tube.

I kept my design simple by using square tiles. Your sundial may be made using any of the techniques in this book, including adding colorant to the cement. You could also design your sundial with an inscription: "Tempus Fugit" (time flies); "Though silent I speak"; "I tell sunny hours only"; "Every hour has its changes"; or your family name. The plastic stamp I used to make the scrollwork imprint is part of a set of stamps used by cake decorators to make letters in icing. It makes perfect lettering easy because the stamps go right into the wet mix. You can also incise the letters directly into the cement using a craft stick. A chisel-shaped tool such as a screwdriver will make attractive calligraphic letters.

MATERIALS

octagonal stepping stone mold
12" x 12" x 1½"
(30cm x 30cm x 38mm)

pencil with eraser

scissors

craft knife

40 vitreous glass tiles, ¾" x ¾"
(18mm x 18mm)

gnomon: I used a 6" (15cm) cast-iron
outdoor plant hook, but 8" (20cm)
would have been even better

1" (25mm) diameter flat rock

ruler

rigid board

dust mask

rubber gloves

7 lbs. (3.2kg)
stepping stone concrete mix

mixing bowl

mixing tool

2 cups (472ml) water

3" (75mm) putty knife

craft stick

optional: scrollwork stamp

1 ➤ Enlarge the pattern. Enlarge the sundial pattern on page 119. For a 12" (30cm) mold, enlarge it on a copy machine 200%. Make two copies.

2 ➤ Make three templates. Place the mold on one enlarged pattern, which will be Template A, centering it over the design. Trace the mold with a pencil. Use scissors to cut out along the traced line. Use a craft knife to cut out and save the geometric cross shape, which you should mark as Template B.

Place the mold on the second copy of the enlarged pattern, centering it over the design. Trace the mold with a pencil and cut along the line. Use a craft knife to cut out the thirteen Roman numerals (just cut a box around each numeral), the large central circle, and a box around the scrollwork at the bottom. This is Template C.

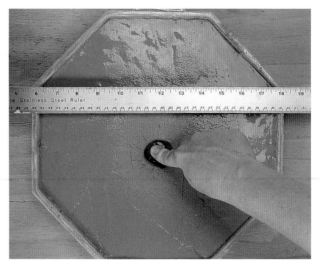

3 ➤ Lay out the tiles on the template. Arrange mosaic tiles on Template B, mixing the colors until you have a pleasing pattern. Leave the middle square blank; this is where the gnomon will be embedded.

4 ➤ Prepare the mix. Place the mold on a board. Put on a dust mask and gloves and prepare the mix as described on pages 23-26. Check the time or set a timer for one hour.

5 ➤ Practice making lines. If this is your first time inscribing lines, see page 36 and make a few lines now. When you're done, smooth and vibrate the mold to erase the practice lines.

6 ➤ Embed a rock prop. The angle of your gnomon should be roughly equal to the latitude of your city. Mine needs to be set at or near 45° because I live in Seattle, which is at 45° latitude. (Bangor, Maine and Toronto, Canada are also at this latitude and would require the same angle.) My plant hook stands at about 60°, and I also want to increase its height, so my solution is to first embed a rock base for my gnomon to lean against. The bottom of the hook will rest on the rock, causing the gnomon to be set at a different angle. Remember, your sundial may not tell the exact time, but setting the gnomon at the correct angle can make it close.

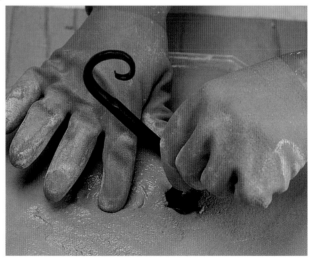

7 ➤ Embed the gnomon. Push the hook into the mix so that it rests on the mold bottom and, if necessary, on the rock. The main arm should extend out of the center of the sundial and reach toward 12 o'clock at a 45° angle.

8 ➤ Fill in the mix. Holding the gnomon with one hand, scrape wet mix to fill in the impression it left. Press down or pat the mix with your gloved hand to even out the surface a little. Hold the hook with one hand and jiggle the mold with the other hand.

9 ➤ Smooth the surface. Try letting go of the hook; it should stand on its own. If not, you need to prop it up so you have both hands free. Use something light that won't sink, such as a tin can. Use your putty knife to smooth the entire surface again.

10 ➤ Use Template A. Position Mold Template A on the wet mix surface, smooth it down and transfer all the mosaic tiles, leaving ⅛" (3mm) between tiles. Work around the hook.

Carefully remove the template. Check to see that the tiles and hook are centered, then embed all the tiles. If the surface needs smoothing or the tiles need leveling, gently tap the sides of the mold. This is your last chance to smooth the surface because you don't want to vibrate the mold after you inscribe the numerals—they will fill in and disappear!

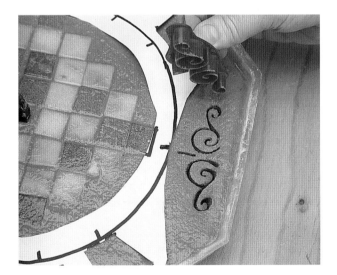

11 ➤ Place Template C. Place Design Template C on the wet mix surface. The numeral boxes should be a minimum of ¼" (6mm) from the edge of the stone and your tiles should be centered in the cut-out circle.

Make the scrollwork impression now, using the scrollwork stamp or drawing the design with a craft stick. If you choose to draw, transfer the design by laying the paper pattern on the mix and making dots with a pointed tool through the design into the mix. Then remove the paper and connect the dots.

12 ➤ Incise the numerals. Use the craft stick to incise the Roman numerals inside the cut-out boxes. Don't incise the horizontal lines yet. Instead of dragging the stick, use an up-and-down motion, making marks about ¼" (6mm) deep. The lines should look dry and crisp. If they are soggy or filling in with water, wait ten minutes and try again.

13 ➤ Finish the numerals. Remove the template and add the horizontal cross strokes at the top and bottom of each numeral. You may need to go over all the lines two or three times to even them out and clean them up. Don't jiggle the mold or the lines will disappear.

Do not try to make or clean up any incised lines after the concrete starts to harden (after about one hour); it may damage or crumble the stone. If you must, do this after 48 hours, using the tip of a bent paper clip. It is still risky because you may chip or flake the concrete.

14 ➤ Set the stone aside to harden for 48 hours. Use the board to move the stone to a safe location. Cover it loosely with plastic and spray it with water after 24 hours.

15 ➤ Clean up the stone. After 48 hours, gently scrub the excess concrete from the tiles, but don't scrub the numerals. Remove the stone from the mold, being careful of the gnomon. Round off the edges as shown on page 39. Rinse the stone well.

16 ➤ Elevate the stone and let it cure. Let the stone cure, elevated on a rack or on pencils, for five more days. Cover it loosely with plastic so that it cures slowly, which makes a sturdier stone. Spray it with water every 24 hours. After five days, the stone will be ready for use.

To enlarge this pattern for a
12" mold, use a copy machine
to enlarge it 200%.

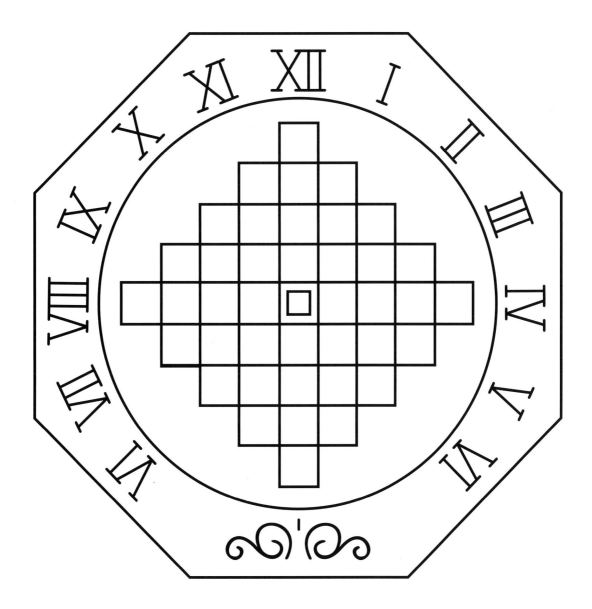

Garden Stakes and Paperweights

Here are some ideas for using up odd tesserae from your other projects. Small mosaics can be paperweights, tiny garden decorations, or with a little ingenuity, fun flower stakes for the garden. "Plant" them in your garden for the summer, then bring them inside for the winter to remind you of warm summer days. I used cookie cutters as molds and found that the lack of a backing was no problem if I set the cookie cutter on a pan covered with sand. If you use a plastic deli container for a mold, just punch a hole in the side for inserting the stake, then plan to cut the mold apart to remove the stone when it has hardened.

All kinds of molds may be used for making paperweights. If you use metal tart pans, aluminum pans or other metal molds, you must paint them with a release agent such as dishwashing liquid. Small plastic deli containers are perfect for making these small mosaics, and you can just throw them away when they become cracked and worn. The instructions show how to make the garden stakes. For paperweights, just follow the same steps except for the ones that show inserting the stake.

MATERIALS

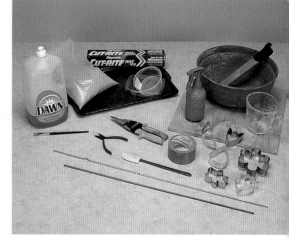

molds:
assorted metal cookie cutters
or deli containers

tin snips

needlenose pliers

duct tape or vinyl tape

metal stakes, 12" to 24"
(30cm to 60cm) long
and ¼" (6mm) diameter

glass nuggets and small pieces
of stained glass

pencil with eraser

scissors

dishwashing liquid, vegetable oil spray
or petroleum jelly

small paintbrush

waxed paper

cookie sheet or rigid board

dust mask

rubber gloves

1½ lbs. (68 kg) (about 2 cups)
stepping stone concrete mix
will make two to three flowers

small mixing bowl

cookie sheet with sand

mixing tool (craft stick)

water

1 cup (288g) fine sand

tablespoon

optional: rubber spatula,
water spray bottle
skid-resistant backing

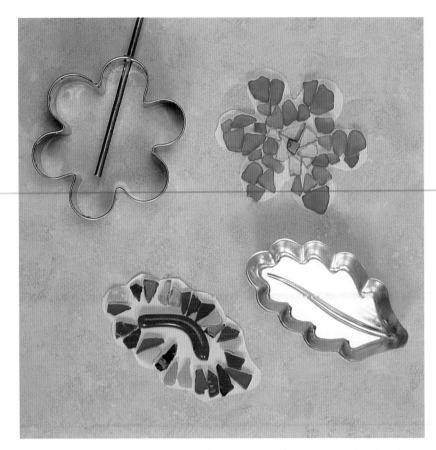

2 ➤ Cut the cookie cutter.
Prepare the cookie cutter mold by cutting a hole in it for the stake. Use tin snips to cut open the cookie cutter. Cut all the way through.

1 ➤ Lay out tesserae. You can lay out your pieces on a paper tracing of your mold, or you can place the tesserae directly into the wet mix without planning ahead.

3 ➤ Cut small notches. On one end at the halfway point cut a tiny notch about ⅛" (3mm) long. Do the same to the other end.

4 ➤ Bend back the corners. Use needlenose pliers to bend the four notch points out so that when you close the cookie cutter there will be a small opening for the stake to fit through. Pinch the sharp points down for safety.

5 ➤ Tape cookie cutter back together. Pinch the cookie cutter closed and insert the stake through the hole. Use duct tape to tape the cookie cutter closed. Insert the stake.

6 ➤ Apply a release agent. Use a small brush to cover the inside of the metal cookie cutter or tart pan with a thin coat of dishwashing liquid or petroleum jelly.

If the tart pan has an indented design on the bottom, as this one has, fill the indentation with sand to keep the wet mix out.

7 ➤ Prepare the baking sheet. Protect the baking sheet with a piece of waxed paper; sprinkle it with a thin layer of sand. Set the cookie cutter on the sand and make sure the stake is level. The edge of my baking sheet did that nicely, but you may need to prop yours up a little more.

Estimate the amount of mix you will need to fill the cookie cutter or mold. If you start with 1 cup (3.4kg) of mix, add 3 table-spoons (45ml) of water and stir well. If needed, add a few drops of water at a time. The thick mix should clump together in your hand and won't seep under the cookie cutter. Check the time or set a timer for one hour.

8 ➤ Fill the molds. Using a rubber spatula or your gloved hand, fill the molds with mix, pushing it down firmly. Push the mix firmly around the stake and smooth the surface. Don't fill it to the top because embedding the pieces will raise the level of mix, possibly overflowing the mold.

While you're embedding, if the surface cracks because the mix is hardening or if the stake is bumped, spray the surface once with water, smooth it with your gloved fingers, and continue embedding.

9 ➤ Embed the tesserae. Transfer the tesserae and use a pencil eraser to embed. Stay ⅛" (3mm) inside the edges. Tap the sides of the mold a few times and lightly smooth the surface with your fingertips.

10 ➤ Set the stones aside to harden for 48 hours. Cover the molds loosely with plastic. Spray with water after 24 hours.

11 ➤ Clean up the stones. After 48 hours, clean the surface as described on page 39. Untape the cookie cutter and carefully peel it away. (If you used a tart pan, turn it upside down and tap it gently.) Small concrete pieces are very fragile at this stage, so handle them with care. Round off the edges and rinse the stones.

12 ➤ Elevate the stones and let them cure. Let the stones cure, elevated on a rack or on pencils, for five more days. Cover them loosely with plastic to slow the curing process. Spray them with water every 24 hours. After five days the garden stakes will be ready to be "planted." The paper-weights need an additional seven days to cure. Cut cork, felt or skid-resistant backing to match the shape of each paperweight and glue it to the bottom.

Gallery

Here are more mosaics that use the same techniques as the projects in this book. Any simple shape can be a source of inspiration for your mosaics. It has been a pleasure sharing my ideas and creations with you. I hope you will spend many fun hours making your own unique mosaics!

Resources

Most mosaic materials can be found at your local craft store. Also look for materials at garden stores, aquarium stores, tile outlets and stained glass stores. Fast-setting concrete is not used in the projects in this book because it sets up too quickly.

CARTER GLASS MOSAIC TILE, DISTRIBUTED BY
HAKATAI ENTERPRISES, INC.
910 Hohokam Dr., Suites 113/114
Tempe, AZ 85281
(888) 667-2429
www.carterglassmosaic.com
➤ Vitreous glass tile in 42 colors

DELPHI STAINED GLASS
3380 East Jolly Road
Lansing, Michigan 48910
(800) 248-2048
www.delphiglass.com
➤ Ceramic tile, smalti, pre-cut stained glass

DIAMONDCRETE
(800) 699-7765
www.diamondcrete.net
➤ Manufacturer of DiamondCRETE fast-setting outdoor cement. Check the web site for stores, plus information about making stepping stones, sealing concrete and Tip of the Month.

DIAMOND TECH INTERNATIONAL
5600 C Airport Blvd.
Tampa, FL 33634
(800) 937-9593
www.dticrafts.com
➤ FlashCrete fast-setting outdoor cement and stained glass pre-cut mosaic pieces

E-Z CRAFT PRODUCTS
2354 Chapman Highway
Sevierville, TN 37876
(800) 311-6529
www.ezcraft.net
➤ Mosaic Mania: packages of color-coordinated stained glass pieces

MILESTONES PRODUCTS COMPANY
15127 NE 24th Street, Suite 332
Redmond, WA 98052
(425) 882-1987
www.milestonecrafts.com
➤ StoneCraft stone mix, color pigment, molds, bags of mosaic glass, ceramic tiles, pebbles, stone lettering stamps and tools, and stepping stone kits

MOSAIC MERCANTILE
P.O. Box 78206
San Francisco, CA 94107
(877) 9-MOSAIC (toll-free)
www.mosaicmercantile.com
➤ Mosaic tile, kits and accessories

MOSAIC TILE SUPPLY
10427 1/2 Unit A Rush Street
South El Monte, CA 91733
http://mosaicsupply.com/
➤ Manufacturer of vintage Italian mosaic tile, tools, stained glass, smalti, and polished abalone for mosaics

MOUNTAINTOP MOSAICS
Elm Street PO Box 653
Castleton, VT 05735
(800) 564-4980
mountaintopmosaics.com/
➤ Vitreous glass mosaic tile, smalti, friendly advice

QUIKRETE COMPANIES
(800) 282-5828
www.quikrete.com
➤ Manufacturer of Concrete Patcher

SEA GLASS, INC.
7000 Boulevard East
Guttenberg, NJ 07093
(973) 344-2222
www.seaglassinc.com
➤ Chunky glass in various colors

SPECTRUM GLASS COMPANY, INC.
P.O. Box 646
Woodinville, WA 98072-0646
(425) 483-6699
www.spectrumglass.com
➤ Manufacturers of art glass

STAINED GLASS WAREHOUSE
97 Underwood Road
Fltecher, NC
(888) 616-7792 (toll-free)
www.stainedglasswarehouse.com
➤ Molds, concrete, stained glass

SUNSHINE GLASSWORKS
111 Industrial Pkwy.
Buffalo, NY 14227
(800) 828-7159
www.sunshineglass.com
➤ Molds, mosaic glass tile, stained glass

TABULARASA
Order smalti diectly from Italy from the Web site:
www.tabularasa.com/

WITS END MOSAICS
5224 West State Road 46, Box 134
Sanford, FL 32771
(407) 323-9122
www.mosaic-witsend.com
➤ Smalti, glass and ceramic tiles, glass nuggets, books and tips

Mosaic Organizations and Web Sites

Mosaic Matters, an online magazine
http://www.asm.dircon.co.uk

British Association for Modern Mosaics
www.bamm.org.uk/index.htm

The Society of American Mosaic Artists
www.scsu.edu/sama

Cole Sonafrank's links to Mosaic Forums, Resources & Studios
http://kokomo.gi.alaska.edu/MosaicLinks.html

Author's Web Site

www.sdonnellydesign.com

Index

Explore the world of crafts with
North Light Books! ➤

Looking for ideas? You're sure to find the perfect mosaic to complement your home or garden, from animals and flowers to classic motifs and geometric patterns. Complete with templates and color variations, this guide offers more than 100 mosaic designs—something for everyone!

1-58180-095-9, paperback, 128 pages

Use the colors, scents and textures of the outdoors to decorate your home in imaginative ways. **Nature Craft** provides easy-to-follow instructions, illustrations and photographs—all the information you need to create unique crafts with readily available natural materials.

0-89134-542-6, paperback, 144 pages

Here are 20 exciting mosaic projects for decorating everything from bathroom walls to garden paths. Clear instruction and step-by-step photos ensure success, whether you're a beginner or an experienced mosaic artist.

1-58180-010-X, paperback with flaps, 128 pages

THESE BOOKS AND OTHER FINE NORTH LIGHT TITLES ARE AVAILABLE FROM YOUR LOCAL ART & CRAFT RETAILER, BOOK-STORE, ONLINE SUPPLIER OR BY CALLING 1-800-221-5831.